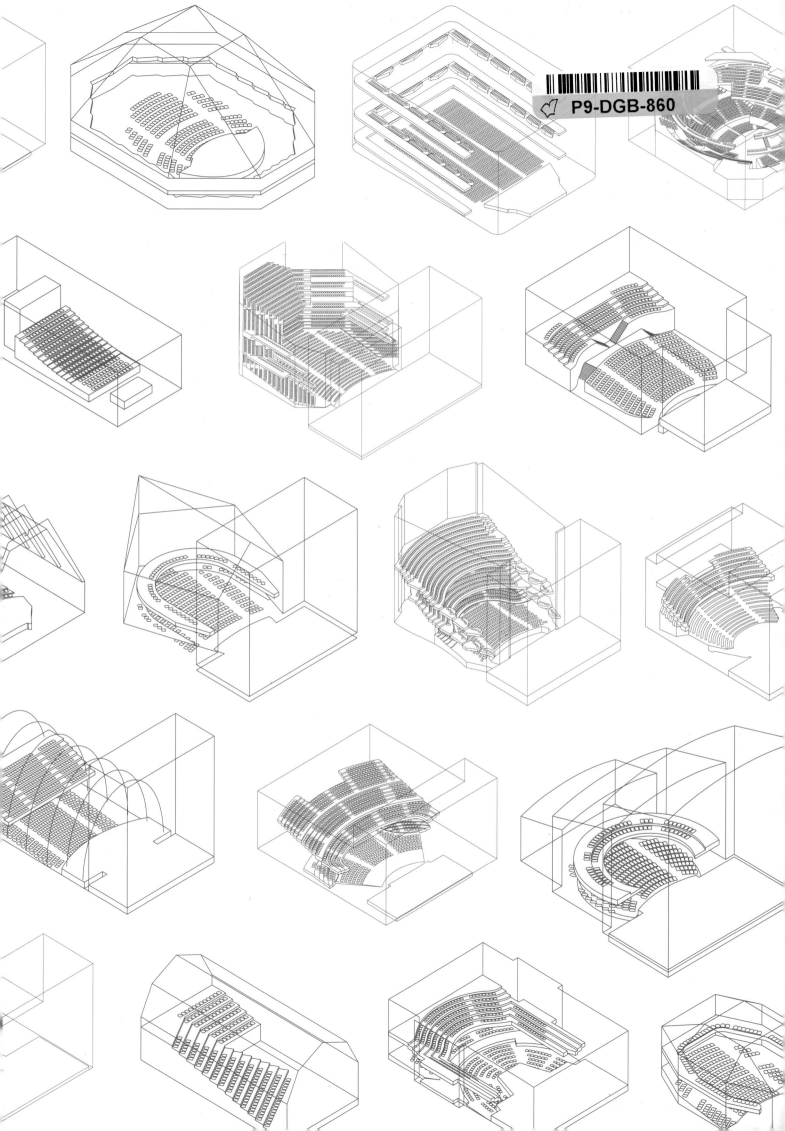

HARDY HOLZMAN PFEIFFER ASSOCIATES

THEATERS

HARDY HOLZMAN PFEIFFER ASSOCIATES

THEATERS

First published in Australia in 2000 by

The Images Publishing Group Pty Ltd

ACN 059 734 431

6 Bastow Place, Mulgrave, Victoria 3170, Australia

Telephone: +(61 3) 9561 5544 Facsimile: +(61 3) 9561 4860

E-mail: books@images.com.au

National Library of Australia Cataloguing-in-Publication Data

    Hardy Holzman Pfeiffer Associates.
    Theaters.

    ISBN 1 86470 027 0.

    1. Theater architecture. 2. Architecture, Modern – 20th
    century. 3. Architecture – Conservation and restoration.
    4. Public spaces. I. Title.

    725.822

Designed by The Graphic Image Studio Pty Ltd
Mulgrave, Australia

Film separations by PageSet Pty Ltd

Printed in Hong Kong

Contents

This volume presents an overview of what makes theater architecture come alive. We recognize there is no particular alchemy which can guarantee this transformation, other than a love of the unexpected and a spirit of adventure, but armed with these, the complex combination of skills required to build a theater has the best chance of success.

The achievement of architecture is like the production of theater: a successful outcome depends upon collaboration. Theater architecture is beholden to an alliance among experts; not only architects but also producers, directors, playwrights, performers, choreographers, conductors, educators, scene and lighting designers, acousticians, and technical consultants. Interaction among their efforts and the place that contains them determines the quality of theatrical experience—for both audience and performer.

Consequently, to enhance this graphic presentation of HHPA's theater architecture we have invited prominent members of the American performing arts community to provide their views about the relationship between theater and architecture. These distinguished contributors have given us their enthusiasm and insight, and we are most grateful. In most cases our authors have written in general about the virtues of a range of theater types, from historic to contemporary, regional to world-renowned, modest to grand. A few have chosen to consider specific HHPA projects, and, in addition, we have included professional comments by the three partners and a director of our theater group.

As times change, new theaters are required. Let us make certain we build them with conviction and delight. Nothing less will do.

Hardy Holzman Pfeiffer Associates
July 1999

Jane Alexander
Actor and former chair of the National
Endowment for the Arts

Phyllis Curtin
Former principal singer of the New
York City Opera, Vienna Staatsoper,
and La Scala Opera

Contributors

Eliot Feld
Choreographer, founder of Ballet
Tech, and co-founder of the Joyce
Theater

Bernard Gersten
Executive producer of Lincoln Center
Theater

Andre Gregory
Director, writer, and actor

Joel Grey
Actor

Paul Marantz
Lighting designer: President, Fisher
Marantz Stone

Dave Shrader
Dean, College of Music, University
of North Texas

Paul Kellogg
General and artistic director of the
New York City Opera and artistic
director of the Glimmerglass Opera

Arthur Mitchell
Founder and artistic director of
the Dance Theatre of Harlem

Jennifer Tipton
Lighting designer

Douglas Kridler
President and executive director
of the Columbus Association for
the Performing Arts

Arthur Penn
Theater and film director

Robin Wagner
Scenic designer

Harvey Lichtenstein
President and executive producer,
BAM

Tony Randall
Actor

Robert Whitehead
Producer and director

Emily Mann
Artistic director and playwright

Frank Rich
Columnist, the Op-Ed page of
The New York Times

Foreword
By Paul Goldberger

The wisest thing ever said to me about the connection between the theater and architecture was a teacher's offhand remark that architecture didn't matter at all. "The greatest theater is done in a barn, not in a palace," he said. I was astonished. I was an eager high school student studying theater for the summer at a local college; architecture and theater were my two loves, and it seemed inconceivable to me that these worlds were not mutually dependent. Surely great architecture enabled great theater; surely the whole experience of going to the theater was bound up in the architectural environment that had been created for it. Wasn't merely being at, say, the Tyrone Guthrie Theater part of the emotional impact? Wasn't Charles Garnier as important to the Paris Opera as any production mounted on that stage? Without a great environment, the theater would certainly suffer.

My teacher was no Philistine—later that summer he lent me a book, a landmark study by the Ford Foundation, which contained eight different proposals for an ideal theater by eight different architects—but he was a realist, and he knew precisely how to rein in the hubris of a teenager who knew too much. He had to make me understand that the theater makes its own magic, and that while architects may nurture it, they do not create it; as often as not, they can stifle it. There is no causal relationship between the quality of the container and the quality of the thing contained. And if the container is too grand, too elaborate, too much of a thing in itself, it can make filling it with the right kind of theater all the more difficult. A great theater recedes from the consciousness of the audience when the lights go down. And it recedes from the consciousness of the players even before then, since it exists to serve them, not to interfere with their creative energies. If it possesses tranquil rehearsal spaces, easy and functional dressing rooms and backstage areas, and a comfortable stage with good sight lines to and from the audience, then it stands a good chance of being a good theater, whatever else it may or may not mean as a work of architecture.

And yet … We all know that a theater is something beyond a purely functional object. A nice green room is all well and good, but there is more to this business than that. It's more than a little disingenuous to suggest that the highest goal of the theater architect is to make a building that will recede from the consciousness of everyone who uses it, to make a building that will aspire to have the qualities of my teacher's imaginary barn. (I will put aside, at least for now, the question of the "black-box" theater, which quite literally does try to be like the barn, a neutral surrounding that all but disappears. There are plenty of black boxes out there, and they serve an essential purpose, but even they have to be set inside of some kind of architectural container.)

But if the theater is to be something other than purely neutral, how does it work as a piece of architecture? How does the architect serve his own need to express himself while not interfering with the director's and the actor's and the playwright's and the composer's and the musician's and the conductor's needs to express themselves? Let me think back again to the question of the connection between architecture and theater, which I, as a presumptuous high school student, was certain worked in only one direction: architecture raising up, even ennobling, the theater. I have now been around long enough to know that the influence works at least as often the other way around: the theater enriches and inspires architecture. The greatest theaters are environments in which the spirit of the theater sets the tone. They are places in which architects have found a point of intersection between the values they have been taught—those of form and space and materials and the cultural resonance that these things have—and the notion of fantasy. If architecture at its most ambitious has a way of being too serious, too self-righteous, the theater is the perfect antidote, for it forces architecture to engage at an experiential level, to come to terms with feeling and emotion. Great architecture always excites our emotions, of course, even as it pretends to be doing something else, but the pleasing thing about theaters is that they do not have to pretend to be doing anything else at all—they can openly solicit our emotions, and the forms can play to them.

I don't mean to say that architecture is an intellectual exercise, and the theater something else. I do mean to say, however, that architecture often purports to be an intellectual exercise, and that the theater, even at its most profound, is more inclined to admit to emotional experience, and that the combination of the two is a wonderful thing for architecture. There are moments when I wonder whether the problem of designing a theater or a concert hall or a performing arts center isn't more like designing a church than a civic assembly hall, since it is an instance of giving concrete form to what is, at bottom, a spiritual experience. Le Corbusier once referred to his great chapel at Ronchamp, France, as "ineffable space," and we might apply that exquisite phrase to all theaters—they exist not to give us answers, but to contain a kind of mystery. In giving that mystery benign and respectful hospitality, they help us find feelings within ourselves.

It is a lot to ask of a building, particularly when you consider the extent to which a theater, even more than a house of worship, has to respond to myriad practical demands: the stage must contain this and that kind of equipment; it must be so large and so high; there must be rehearsal spaces and offices and dressing rooms and technical equipment and public areas that will not only give the audience enough room but also prepare it emotionally for the experience to follow. Most important of all, both the theater and the house of worship exist, paradoxically, to symbolize at once community and privacy; they are places in which people come together, and celebrate the fact of their coming together, yet they are there to experience things that are very much their own. In most of the world, reality imposes itself upon us, and we escape into private fantasies. In the theater, the construct

that surrounds us is, in part, itself a fantasy, an architectural environment made to symbolize a kind of magic. If it is working, a great piece of theater architecture, like the theater itself, uses this fantasy to help us escape into a more knowing and wise reality.

So it can be said, I think, of most of the work of Hardy Holzman Pfeiffer Associates, which has emerged from the belief that the values of the theater and the values of architecture need not be inconsistent—indeed, that they can come together and enrich one another profoundly. These architects have always valued fantasy, but never at the expense of tectonic truths. Their architecture is not frivolous, and neither is it weighed down by abstract theory. For all that it takes enthusiastic note of the past, it is committed to being of this time and this place. It is emotional, but it is not sentimental. The theaters of HHPA represent a kind of architecture that embraces experience and honors real life. Fantasy here is used in much the way that Picasso had in mind when he spoke of art as a lie that leads us to truth: such is the make believe of HHPA's theater architecture, a set of illusions designed to heighten actuality. Like the theater itself, this is architecture that celebrates imagination above all.

Introduction
By Debra Waters

n each of our 32 years of practice, Hardy Holzman Pfeiffer Associates has engaged in the process of planning, designing, or constructing a theater. In total we have developed more than 115 places for music, dance, drama, opera, and film. Our designs range from formal arena, thrust, or proscenium stages to informal studio spaces. Many are flexible in order to permit a variety of performance types. Others are theatrically and acoustically tailored to meet the specific needs of a particular production company. Our clients include non-profit organizations, public agencies, private commercial entities, and educational institutions. Their

Taylor Theater © Norman McGrath

New Lafayette Theater II © Norman McGrath

New Lafayette Theater II © Norman McGrath

Thrust-stage, Taylor Theater © Norman McGrath

theaters serve as catalysts for the rejuvenation of urban areas, create tourist destinations in rural areas, contribute to the synergy of emerging cultural districts, nurture the artistic maturity of students, draw the public to university campuses, or enhance fledgling arts organizations. The diversity and depth of our work underscores a fundamental axiom of theater architecture: it cannot be created by formula. Each theater must be the product of an individual, fresh approach to design.

The first HHPA performance space to open was the Arts Center at Simon's Rock College of Bard, in 1967. Here we reused an existing barn to allow for an irregularly shaped 200-seat theater which had distinct seating sections set at two angles to the stage, whose rear wall was open to views of the Berkshire hills. A year later we converted an old ballroom in New York's central Harlem into the New Lafayette Theater II. It was the first new theater built there since Orson Welles' Mercury. At the same time we designed a new asymmetrical thrust-stage theater for Cincinnati's Playhouse in the Park. In 1969, our design of the Taylor Theater, in a carriage barn, surrounded an elevated thrust-stage with five rows of stepped seating. The Emelin Theater, which opened in 1972, featured an open-end stage with a curved asymmetrical seating section and a mezzanine, which afforded excellent sight lines. That same year we used a pre-engineered industrial building system to create an offset audience configuration for Phillips Exeter Academy's Fisher Theater. Boettcher Concert Hall, completed in 1978, was the first concert hall in America whose seating completely surrounded the stage, challenging the traditional "shoe-box" relationship between audience and orchestra.

These projects are the precursors to others found in this publication. The 30 featured completed projects and those currently on HHPA computer screens amplify many of the design principles that governed this earlier work; most notably, the application of innovative materials or the use of unconventional seating configurations which result in intimate spaces, applauded by audiences and performers alike.

Our theater projects presently in design or construction continue this legacy of program diversity and site-specific design. The new 600-seat theater and 200-seat IMAX film theater at the Whitaker Center for Science and the Arts caters for local arts organizations in Harrisburg, Pennsylvania. The city of Columbus, Georgia, and Columbus State University will share a 2,000-seat multi-purpose hall, a recital hall, and an experimental theater as part of RiverCenter, a new 230,000-square-foot, joint-use arts complex. Programming and master planning for the new Long Wharf Theatre in New Haven,

Emelin Theater © Norman McGrath

Grand Foyer circa 1932, Radio City Music Hall
© Courtesy of Radio City Music Hall Archives

View from stage, Phillips Exeter Academy's Fisher Theater © Norman McGrath

Rockettes circa 1932, Radio City Music Hall
© Courtesy of Radio City Music Hall Archives

Auditorium circa 1932, Radio City Music Hall © Courtesy of Radio City Music Hall Archives

South and east facades, Whitaker Center for Science and the Arts © Michael Moran

Connecticut, and the Trinity Rep of Providence, Rhode Island, will allow for greater artistic opportunities while contributing to each city's goal of becoming a recognized cultural destination.

Our current work also extends to interpretive restorations designed to insure the profitability and ongoing success of beloved theaters by addressing the requirements of contemporary building codes and the needs of contemporary audiences. Our restoration of the 5,900-seat Radio City Music Hall, in New York City, will re-establish this national landmark as one of the world's premier entertainment facilities. Redevelopment of the vacant Hippodrome, in Baltimore, Maryland, along with two adjacent historic buildings, will make the Hippodrome Performing Arts Center the only venue in that city capable of accommodating the latest Broadway shows.

HHPA's ability to create theaters that give delight to visitors and pride to owners and artists is a direct result of the partners' concern for the excitement of performance and the complexity of theater use. In his essay, Hugh Hardy sees creative performance as sustenance for civilized society. He addresses the qualities of a theater's shape and character that support performance and inspire audiences. Malcolm Holzman believes intimacy is garnered as much from the architectural nuances of a theater, as from the physical relationship of patron to performer. Norman Pfeiffer broadens the definition of theater to encompass its contribution to community development. Stewart Jones, a director of

HHPA's theater group, considers the financial, social, and aesthetic dimensions theaters must address in the twenty-first century.

Complementing their insights are illustrations of HHPA projects. Among these are diagrams of theater configurations that allow for a variety of presentation types, public spaces that encourage people-watching, exteriors that are inviting, and auditoriums that draw audience and artist together. We hope the observations of all who have contributed to this publication and the work itself will rouse the imagination and daring that make great theater possible.

Elevation, RiverCenter for the Performing Arts, rendering by David Purceil

Elevation, Hippodrome Performing Arts Center, rendering by Lee Dunnette

When Two Worlds Become One

By Hugh Hardy, FAIA

The characteristics of good theater architecture are elusive. We recognize great theaters when we see them, and it is obvious that such places contribute to the power of communication between audience and performer. But defining what makes architectural success possible is difficult, complex, and abstract. It lies beyond surface appearance or matters of decoration and detail. Beyond each building's obvious need for enclosure lies the necessity of creating a place where the audience and performer can be joined in shared understanding. Though these participants arrive from different worlds, they are united by common expectation, and when a memorable performance takes place they come together with an intense intimacy. Good theater architecture must support and encourage this relationship. It must offer the audience a heightened sense that noteworthy and immediate events are taking place. Although performance is transitory, at its best it becomes the stuff of indestructible memory. To create such impressions, theater architecture must be able to make the auditorium disappear so that during performance only the actors rule, and it must be able to make performers appear larger than life-size. It should give actors a sense of great closeness to the assembled, offering an embrace of expectant faces.

We are told that with "two boards and a passion" theater can be presented anywhere. Of course, performance can take place without any fixed relation between audience and performer, or even any seats. But how is it possible to mold the auditorium so that communication between audience and performer reaches its highest level? Although aesthetics are an essential ingredient, we must first investigate the basic seating configuration of the auditorium if we are to

understand what makes good theater architecture. No amount of décor can offer success unless the seating is properly shaped.

The process of shaping the audience chamber should create a spatial emphasis that focuses attention toward the stage. Typically, theater interiors are organized with fixed seats in rows or layers, and this placement of the audience determines how the performers are seen. In turn, it influences where movement takes place on stage and establishes the relation between performers and scenery. For instance, theater in the round presents performers as free-standing figures without a background of scenic elements, while proscenium productions present performers as part of a scenic picture. Although each relationship has its supporters and opponents, both are viable.

Whatever the audience–performer relationship, auditorium design begins with the organization of the seating levels. These must be arranged to give the best possible sight lines for the audience with the shortest distance to the stage. Many relationships between audience and performer are possible, some formal and fixed, others informal and flexible. Choosing the right configuration is an exercise in three dimensions. For instance, the fan-shaped auditorium often used in schools was actually developed in movie theaters for viewing large images whose field of vision is controlled by the camera. As a result, it places seats in the remote corners of the plan, locating them too far from the stage for live performances. Stacking the audience in layers with one, two, or three balconies can create intimacy for some but creates steep sight lines for the upper reaches of the auditorium. If wrapped too tightly toward a proscenium, this pattern can also produce poor visibility of the stage. A large balcony efficiently holds

many people, but it divides the audience in two, causing those sitting high up in its generous expanse to have a different experience of a presentation than those located below, in the orchestra. Steeply raked orchestra levels produce alpine configurations in the balcony, and these create odd viewing angles.

To add to this complexity, the character of contemporary productions is changing. Even in traditional proscenium theaters, contemporary directors often prefer to join viewer and performer in a single space, pressing productions forward into the audience beyond the curtain line. Doing so results in a more immediate relationship, but can greatly diminish the quality of sight lines. The design of new proscenium theaters must therefore recognize this trend and shape sight lines to accommodate performers in front of the proscenium. Although the popularity of thrust-stage presentations is declining, their placement of performers and audience in the same space creates great intimacy and continues to be favored by some directors. Despite its intimacy, theater in the round, where audiences completely surround the stage, now has even fewer advocates, because of its staging difficulties and scenic limitations for all but the smallest capacities.

For producers and audiences alike, theater is an encounter with the unexpected. Because the requirements for each presentation are different, flexibility is another basic goal of its architecture. It is far easier, however, to change production style and focus than to change audience seating. Over time the fixed, frontal relationship of proscenium theaters has proven remarkably flexible. It continues to be favored even though its seating is permanent. Studio theaters with a capacity of fewer than 100 can use loose chairs to shape playing areas, but theaters with larger movable seating areas

Balcony detail, Whitaker Center for Science and the Arts © Michael Moran

Sunoco Theater, Whitaker Center for Science and the Arts © Michael Moran

seldom change configuration. The cost, technical complexity, and difficulty of making large seating banks movable and the labor required to relocate, redirect, and refocus lighting equipment or rearrange scenery prevents this form of malleability.

In short, there is no right or wrong relationship between audience and performer. Each has its virtues, each its limitations. Each must be considered in relation to the programmed capacity, production style, and scale of intended presentation. For instance, a wide proscenium may be ideal for spectacle, but the resulting seating configuration will hinder intimate drama. A thrust-stage may be perfect for the presentation of plays, but is awkward for opera. Whatever the production approach, the hope is to strike a balance between distance from the stage and angle of viewing so that the individual members of the audience feel themselves part of a whole. The goal is to insure audience members are aware of each other, sensing they are gathered to witness an event together.

Although an auditorium's aesthetic character is of secondary importance to its shape, it is nonetheless an essential part of the audience experience, especially before performance, when anticipation is at its height. In conventional designs, the theater's floor, walls, and ceiling form an integrated whole. Traditional houses use large geometric gestures to unify these surfaces. This remains a valid design device which, properly employed, can create great intimacy. In contemporary designs it is also possible to contrast these elements of enclosure to create a more dissonant design vocabulary. Past theaters relied upon representational decoration to create a sense of special occasion. Garlands and putti, classical motifs, murals, and statuary were all pressed into service. The resulting interiors contain their audiences in a lavish realm of gilt and plush, one removed from everyday experience. Here, the proscenium frame and lushly draped main curtain present the stage as a view into another world. Contemporary theaters, on the other hand, strive to become part of everyday experience and often use the paraphernalia of structure, lighting, technical equipment, and rigging to create a working environment whose excitement comes not from the romance of tradition but from seeing the space transformed by performance.

Whatever the stylistic devices used, ornament is needed to provide human scale. Present-day techniques of surface ornamentation can reinterpret traditional décor or offer entirely new materials and lighting effects. Any approach, however, must frankly acknowledge the presence of theater technology in the auditorium. Contemporary productions continue to advance technical ganglia into audience areas with catwalks, lighting equipment, and rigging. All these production necessities can be used as design features to form an important design element of the interior. Because the location of this equipment varies from production to production, efforts to obscure it fail, yielding far worse results than accepting its bristling patterns as part of the theater's design.

In the 1920s, America's devotion to the movies created some incredibly large and ornate performance halls. Because these places were dependent upon amplified sound, they have only recently come into use again as hosts to large-scale touring productions of Broadway musicals. Because in these movie houses films were shown continuously without intermission, they did not require large public spaces, and stage presentations were limited to vaudeville. However, the main architectural task of these immense rooms, undertaken with gusto by a host of eclectic architects, was to relate the relatively small scale of the picture images to the vast audiences for whom they were shown. In the process, these designers concocted a spirited review of architectural history whose encyclopedic scope has not been seen before or since. However reviled by purists, such plaster fantasies present instructive ideas about the use of ornamental detail to bring large-scale interiors down to human proportions. Their boisterous results and fearless scavenging of history offer little direct assistance to today's design practitioners, but the varied range of the forms and colors used do offer splendid examples of how ornament and lighting can contribute to a sense of occasion.

Alas, for those who need rules, there is no universal dictum to apply to good theater design other than the hope these rooms will enhance the artists' ability to seize the imagination of their audiences. In theater, whatever the design vocabulary used, architecture must learn to be supportive, not dominant, dedicated to forging an inseparable bond between audience and performer. As the variety of theaters found in this book illustrates, there are many ways to achieve this goal. No single solution can please all. But a sense of occasion and delight is required. The buildings which celebrate theater as splendid public ritual are the most likely to succeed. In fact, nothing less will do.

Bridging the Gap

By Malcolm Holzman

Auditorium, Ramapo College, Berrie Center for the Performing and Visual Arts © Michael Moran

Have you ever seen a concert-goer one-third of the way through a performance gazing at the details of the auditorium's walls or ceiling? I do at almost every event I attend. This scrutiny is not simply a way to pass the time; it can be a valuable part of the evening's experience. Despite appearances to the contrary, such audiences are not being distracted by architecture; they are actually finding a way to place the details of a room in scale with the performers on stage and the larger audience chamber. Audiences connect with performers not only through the production itself, but also through their perception of how the performance fits into its surroundings. A sense of intimacy results from this measuring process. Without it, a theater visit—no matter how pleasant the amenities or the company of friends—will not be successful. Auditorium design is important in achieving this rapport.

The creation of a bond between audience and performer has numerous precedents. The semicircular seating at Epidauros, the elliptical seating at Palladio's Teatrico Olympico, and the frontal seating of Vienna's Musikvereinsaal lock the two groups together in a special relationship. These memorable, intimate spaces were shaped by individual designers for communal enjoyment.

The presentation on an auditorium stage may be considered high art, but not always the architecture that surrounds it. When they opened, neither Charles Garnier's Paris Opera House of the last century nor John Eberson's atmospheric movie palaces of the late 1920s was considered worthy of critical architectural evaluation. These auditoriums, with gold-leafed caryatids supporting a balcony, or Spanish-inspired courtyards under an evening sky, were initially thought to be pandering to popular taste. Time has altered this judgment. Today these theaters are valued for their intimacy, decorative opulence, and sense of place. Certain building types, among them theaters, seldom fit the stylistic classifications that interest

Seating and rail detail, Middlebury College, Center for the Arts © Norman McGrath

Lobby, Ramapo College, Berrie Center for the Performing and Visual Arts © Michael Moran

critics of a given era, and it usually takes succeeding generations using these buildings continuously for performance to elicit meaningful judgments about an auditorium's adequacy.

More theaters were built worldwide in the 1990s than at any time since the 1920s movie palace boom. And in that time, more money was spent to construct a square foot of theater space than a square foot of any other building type except, perhaps, a hospital or prison. Today's theaters differ in significant ways from their predecessors: in patron comfort, technological sophistication, acoustics, proximity to parking, and inclusion of facilities like shops and art galleries. Many of today's auditoriums have seating capacities of 2,000 or more, a necessity to offset the costs of presenting touring shows, symphony, and opera. The farthest seat may be 120 feet from the stage in these theaters, more than the length of a professional basketball court. Numerous balcony seats are located above the height of the proscenium arch, forcing patrons to view the performance at a steep angle. Creating a sense of intimacy in these huge halls is the true challenge to the theater designer.

The decor of contemporary theaters bears little resemblance to the ornamental cherubs, garlands, and swags that adorned proscenium arches and surrounding boxes until the 1950s. It has been five decades since matched wood paneling, streamlined lighting coves, and stylized wall sconces gave proportion to auditorium surfaces. Since mid-century, the predominant style for auditoriums has been Modernism, the underlying ethos of which is the reduction of design features to an absolute minimum. In such arrangements, any indication that a room is constructed of distinct incremental parts must be made invisible. We cannot (nor do we wish to) turn back the clock; the appearance of an auditorium must stem directly from contemporary methods of construction and its detail. Theater design needs to move beyond recent reductionist attitudes.

During the last 20 years, research projects, conducted mainly by individuals interested in theater technics, have delved into evaluating the world's most successful auditoriums. Studies of physical phenomena related to acoustics, sight lines, and seating comfort have resulted in improvements to these areas in new auditoriums. Architectural design analyses have focused on theater form, and, in turn, have led to the consensus that good symphonic music halls are usually shaped like shoe boxes and good opera houses are more or less horseshoe-shaped cylinders. Throughout this era, small theater formats with regular geometric shapes have been inflated proportionately to 2,000-seat presentation rooms. This transformation has shown that geometry alone cannot provide an intimate setting at this enlarged scale.

Making public buildings has been HHPA's specialty for more than three decades. Our auditoriums have been constructed episodically, their design based on a range of project-specific determinants, varying from presentation formats to the incorporation of regional materials. There have been digressions for specialized uses and to accommodate existing conditions. There were awkward moments but also flashes of inspiration and beauty. During some periods the firm was making new theaters and restoring old ones at the same time. Working in auditoriums ranging in age from 20 to 100 years has allowed us to study how earlier designers used the mechanics and magic of theater to join audience with performer in lively and focused environments. We neither overthrow previous generations' design concerns nor copy their surface decorations. Rather, HHPA incorporates and translates effective methods from all eras without being overwhelmed by style. Our new auditoriums are informed by history; the restored ones are kept true to their original spirit and made technologically current. The key to making good theaters is the knowledge that spontaneity and intimacy must bridge the gap between performer and audience.

Auditorium, Vilar Center for the Arts © Foaad Farah

Theater: a building for dramatic purposes
(Webster's Dictionary).

Theater: Building Community and the Public Realm

By Norman Pfeiffer

Lobby, Vilar Center for the Arts © Foaad Farah

This rather simple definition needs adjustment. "Theater" no longer refers only to auditoriums where orchestra and balcony seating, proscenium stages, and chandeliered ceilings usher audiences into a magical world. "Going to the theater" now implies much more than passive attendance at a performance; it signifies participation in the social life of our cities. Today, theater-goers are likely to arrive early for pre-performance snacks in the lobby or dinners in the neighborhood; to stay late for post-theater discussions; to attend lectures on a Saturday afternoon; to visit the plaza for a midday lunch concert; or to take a youngster to a children's puppet theater production in the informal outdoor amphitheater. Young people appreciate the arts in greater and more diverse numbers just as older generations are experiencing a renewed interest in cultural offerings. While the resulting proliferation of theaters and performing arts centers offers architects the opportunity to build buildings, it also offers public agencies, non-profit organizations, and artists the opportunity to build community.

In his 1967 opening address at the 12th International Theater Institute conference in New York, Arthur Miller said, "We are a small, huddling group of inadequate theaters and a growing group of impressive buildings springing up all over the country, without a vision, without a concept of which man is the center."

But over the past 30-plus years, a vision has developed: one in which "man," the audience, is invited by theater spaces to gather socially, to celebrate cultural diversity, and to help create neighborhoods. The vision takes many forms, among them an exchange between the artistic pursuits of students and those of working professionals. Whether theaters bring students into the heart of downtown or community audiences go to the center of campus, this intermixing of the academic with the residential and business lives of a city is having profound effects—artistically, financially, and socially. The influx of students into downtown is creating more vibrant centers during the day and on week nights, when traditional theaters in smaller cities are typically dark. In addition, the opportunity for students to work with professionals—on stage and behind the scenes—bolsters their educational experience and often their confidence as they move forward in their careers. This intermixing also strengthens ties between the community and academia, as residents participate in a growing variety of collegiate activities.

Just as museums and public libraries are taking on expanded roles—offering venues for public events, educational activities, food, retail, and outdoor events—theater lobbies, having traditionally had the singular function of "containing" audiences during intermissions, are taking on a life of their own. Now these vibrant spaces are in use 24 hours a day and are host to informal gatherings, banquets, receptions, meetings, art exhibitions, fund-raising activities, and casual dining before and after performances. Even the stage, once the sole province of performers, is assuming a new, though secondary, role. It, too, is used for special events these days, and has become a valuable resource during periods when theaters would otherwise be dark.

In many cities, theater complexes are part of the public realm, with their lobbies and public spaces serving as internal streets and walkways. The surrounding outdoor areas are also increasingly important, now that their plazas and open spaces are expressly designed to connect to the life and movement of the city. A range of activities, from impromptu musical performances to children's theater, arts festivals, and galas, occurs here, too.

Finally, theaters today are being asked to make an architectural contribution to the city—either to blend into the aesthetic fabric of a community or to stand as icons, symbols of artistic and civic achievement. In its contextual form, architecture serves as a backdrop against which the life of the city is played out. But icons must earn this distinction. They have the ability to give identity to communities, to serve as focal points in their own right, or to participate in neighborhood rebirth.

Perhaps the definition of theater today might read:

Theater: an urban architectural phenomenon for the dramatic purpose not only of performance but also of the building of community.

May Gallery for Visual Arts, Vilar Center for the Arts © Foaad Farah

Twenty-first Century Challenges for the Theater Architect

By Stewart Jones

Sunoco Theater, Whitaker Center for Science and the Arts © Michael Moran

Like the beginning of this century, when vaudeville houses sprang up across the country, the year 2000 will be ushered in by a theater building boom. New construction and renovation of every kind of theater, from small repertory facilities to vast performing arts centers, is taking place countrywide. Theater is being redefined by a new generation of artistic directors, and the buildings that follow must respond.

Where theaters used to be built to offer performances only, they have lately assumed a far greater social and educational role. Along with libraries and museums, they must now relate to their physical and cultural surroundings, serve as destinations for people of all ages, and accommodate day- and night-time activities. Frequently, urban renewal is also part of the agenda. In conceiving a project, the theater's artistic brain trust and design team must be clear about the institution's vision and the ways in which the building's occupants want to be represented in the community. Because the results of these efforts will have a lasting impact on the public and owners alike, philosophical thinking about these buildings should occur early. Once the process starts, choices evaporate.

As a result of the theater's expanded community presence, performing arts facilities increasingly share space with other public venues, such as science centers, IMAX theaters, arenas for popular entertainment, and film-screening rooms, which can offer related programs. To attract ever greater numbers

Lobby detail, Whitaker Center for Science and the Arts
© *Michael Moran*

of patrons and to accommodate their needs, these facilities offer amenities unheard of during most of this century, such as ample lobby space, retail shops for book and records, cafes, and full-service restaurants. A challenge for 21st century architects is positioning theaters in buildings that contain so many competing public areas. From a more practical point of view, sharing spaces and services reduces capital investment and keeps operational expenses down.

It is inevitable that this new spate of theater building will quickly exhaust sources of revenue and that the allocation of monies will be scrutinized ever more closely. Business plans, with realistic projections of needs and attendance, have never been more important. Board members want to know the need is solid; the program, plan, and design are appropriate; costs are realistic; and funding is optimistic. In most cases, the days of "build it and they will come" are over.

Once all parties clearly understand the financial as well as the social and cultural implications of restoring a theater or building a new one, they can turn their attention to the design process. Managing assets is just as crucial in this phase as in the others. Arriving at an estimated cost based on a written program, before any drawings are produced, encourages careful evaluation of the architectural agenda. This assessment is the most important step in the cost management process, because it allows the most change; once drawings begin and the design develops, the window of opportunity starts to close.

For the presentation of performing arts to be successful, a multi-disciplinary team approach is required. Architect, theater consultant, acoustician, engineer, user, and operator all collaborate in the process. The architect, responsible for disseminating, coordinating, and focusing the design team's enormous energies, must also be able to clearly communicate designs to the client.

Weaving new venues into urban and suburban fabric and enhancing the performing arts' role in the community will be crucial to theaters' success in the 21st century. The design team would do well to remember, however, that the performance on stage remains of paramount importance. In connecting the generations and the centuries, performance has the greatest reach of all.

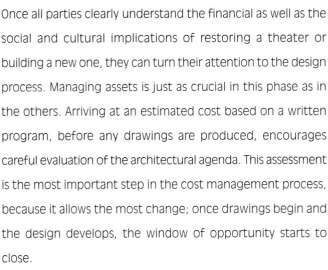

Lower level lobby, Whitaker Center for Science and the Arts © *Michael Moran*

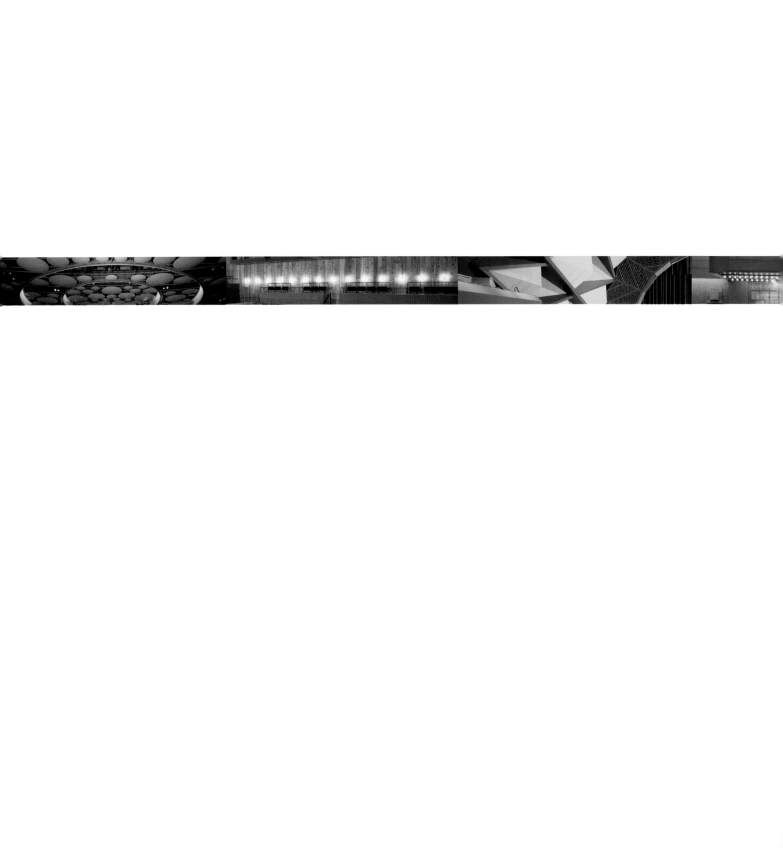

Selected
Essays and Theaters

A GOOD THEATER GATHERS

Arthur Penn

The elaborate adornments of box seats, great chandeliers, sconces, and orchestra pits that embellish most theater auditoriums condemn the audience to the isolation of pedestrians beneath umbrellas in a downpour. The stage itself is too often buried behind the luxurious velvets of a royal funeral, designating us as groundling onlookers at a majestic burial.

Preparing a disparate group of individuals to convert themselves willingly into an audience is an essential requirement in the creation of a good theater. The embrace of an original theater should beguile us to set aside the shelter of self-defence and lure us toward mutual mystery. As the members of the gathering surrender their individuality to the embrace of a felicitous surrounding, they begin a connection with others. It is that connection of shared anticipation of the unknown that fulfills the first condition of a theater: the assembled people have become an audience.

One hopes that is to be followed swiftly by the unfolding of human events on the stage that quicken the senses and capture our audience in its thrall. Neither the forbidding barrier of many stages nor an arrogant, exaggerated thrust of performing space will win the shy and skittish audience. Recent horrors of stages filled with engines and machinery distort the experience of theater into a fairground of whirling devices with the persons assembled watching passively and distantly. That is not a theater; it is a bad carnival on expensive real estate.

An embrace is mutual. The theater where the play happens should offer itself with tenderness. A good theater gathers. It emits an atmosphere of mysterious anticipation into which it draws the audience and then disappears into itself, allowing the collective imagination to become the structure.

Simon's Rock College of Bard Arts Center

Simon's Rock College of Bard Arts Center
© Norman McGrath

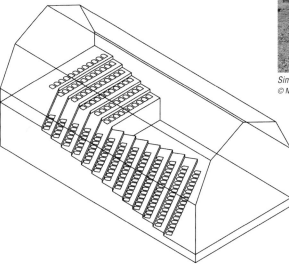

View from stage, Simon's Rock College of Bard Arts Center © Norman McGrath

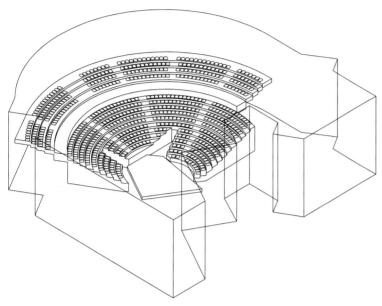

Playhouse in the Park:
Robert S. Marx Theater

Catwalk, Playhouse in the Park,
Robert S. Marx Theater
© Norman McGrath

Façade, Playhouse in the Park, Robert
S. Marx Theater © Norman McGrath

Lobby, Playhouse in the Park, Robert S. Marx
Theater © Norman McGrath

Auditorium, Playhouse in the Park, Robert
S. Marx Theater © Norman McGrath

THEATRICAL ARCHITECTURE

Arthur Mitchell

While most theaters are built with the comfort of the audience in mind, they must also consider the performers, creating a "safe place" in which they can take risks.

The stage should be flexible, with the ability to go from a proscenium to a thrust in a short time. The floor must be sprung to help dancers avoid injury. The stage, or a portion of it, should be on a lift, allowing presentation on more than one level at a time. Adequate wing and fly spaces are essential, allowing for large-scale work and multiple set pieces.

Comfortable dressing rooms close to the stage should be equipped with showers and private restroom facilities. It is extremely important that the sound system allow stage managers, technical crew, and artists to communicate with one another. A rehearsal room of the same dimensions as the stage is essential when a company is changing its repertory, and allows one set of dancers to prepare while another is on the stage. A canteen, much in favor in Europe, permits eating and drinking backstage and aids in creating a "home" for the artists.

In a well-designed theater, the stage and artists make up one half of a giant circle, the audience the other. The two should feel they go together, as if they were reaching toward one another. It is this unity that allows a performance to transcend its practical realities and attain the level of art.

Lobby, American Film Institute, Washington, DC © Norman McGrath

Auditorium, American Film Institute, Washington, DC © Norman McGrath

Auditorium, American Film Institute, Los Angeles, CA
© Norman McGrath

American Film Institute

Adelphi University, Robert G. Olmsted Theater

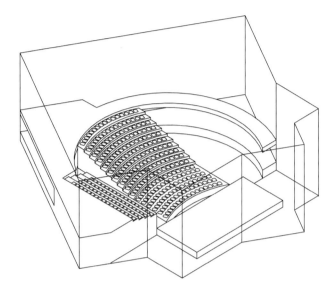

Adelphi University, Robert G. Olmsted Theater © Norman McGrath

Adelphi University, Robert G. Olmsted Theater
© Norman McGrath

View toward stage, Adelphi University, Robert G. Olmsted
Theater © Norman McGrath

LIGHT IN THE THEATER

Paul Marantz

The title of this essay is deliberately ambiguous. Are we to discuss light and theater architecture, or light as used on the stage? Is there a difference? Are these questions even relevant in these last hours of the 20th century, when the fragile distinction between reality and artifice has blurred further, when simulacra of the monuments of the world are rising in Las Vegas, and life on the screen (movie, TV, computer) has displaced much of life in the three-dimensional world?

How are we to make, and light, theater buildings, when the activities they traditionally contained have escaped into the "real" world? My partner, the noted stage lighting designer Jules Fisher, is asked to light a live entertainment conceived as a free attraction for the public spaces of a shopping mall. The sneaker shop in that mall will also use stage lighting effects, as will the restaurant, the teen clothing outlets, and the mall's exterior. As the artifice of the stage has clothed more of our daily activities, what are we to make of those buildings that traditionally enclosed (and therefore ennobled) that kind of experience? The challenge to design uniquely identifiable theater buildings grows more complicated when the rest of the built environment borrows the theater's language. These are a lighting designer's concerns, because light in theater buildings, as in all of architecture, interprets those buildings for the viewer. By emphasis or concealment, kineticism or serenity, coolness or warmth, light communicates a building's meaning.

Historically, theaters were seen as part of the collection of grand civic buildings that characterized urban centers. Their design language was Neoclassical; they could have been mistaken for courthouses, city halls, or libraries. Later, advertising, in the form of

North façade, Orchestra Hall © Norman McGrath

Concert hall from second balcony, Orchestra Hall © Norman McGrath

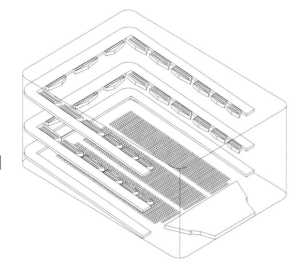

Orchestra Hall

Concert hall from first balcony, Orchestra Hall © Norman McGrath

marquees, banners, building signs, and poster boxes, began to distinguish theater buildings by day. The incandescent lamp, as adjunct to advertising, created a night-time character for theaters, giving them special prominence in the urban fabric. Theater buildings began to look unique and, therefore, identifiable. In early photographs of Times Square and other urban centers, the theater buildings stand out clearly.

Inside, public spaces include the foyers and lobbies, perhaps a cafe or bar, and the hall itself. The generosity of the peripheral spaces depends on the programmatic goals of the sponsors, the size of the site, and the budget. Theater attendance is a social experience, and the public spaces provide the venue for this. If these areas are visually linked to the exterior, the pre-show crowd is another indicator of the building's purpose—good advertising. Lighting here must enhance this most important social function. Live performances, with one or two intermissions providing time for audience interaction, promote a sense of community. We illuminate these areas using the same criteria we would employ for any first-class public gathering space. Warm, sparkling, flattering light is always appropriate. These characteristics are achievable in every architectural idiom.

However welcoming the secondary public spaces, they remain a prologue to the performance spaces. We attend live performances to share in a special, heightened experience, outside the daily routine. We're filled with anticipation, and perhaps a little anxiety—will the event be worth our time, interest, and money?

The entire physical environment should enhance these feelings. We want our excitement reflected in the room. In a concert hall, musicians are coming on stage and tuning up while the audience is reviewing the program. In the theater, the set may be visible, dramatically lit; actors may already inhabit it. Even in a traditional

Original multi-level lobby, Orchestra Hall © Norman McGrath

Renovated ground level lobby, Orchestra Hall © George Heinrich

Boettcher Concert Hall

North facade with galleria in foreground, Boettcher Concert Hall © Norman McGrath

proscenium theater the curtain is "warmed" with stage lighting. Something is about to happen. And yet we're still happy to be in the company of our fellow audience members; we're not yet ready to lose ourselves to the performance.

Our minds wander. Look at those little kids! What could their parents be thinking, bringing them to a show like this? That woman must love Beethoven quartets. I've seen her before at this series.

In the traditional classic proscenium theater, gilded and glittering, with red velour seats and curtain, there is a design dilemma that naturally engages the question of lighting. Whatever lies behind the curtain is a secret, and since the theater will be dark before the curtain rises, we'll have a chance to clear our memory of the room's architecture and be ready for the architecture of the play. If the director wants to involve us earlier, the curtain will be raised and the set lighted, as if the show's begun before we arrived. That gilded room is now a liability, distracting us. Our director would prefer a less committed space, one he could take over with less effort. The front portion of more than one Broadway house has been overpainted with neutral dark color to solve this problem. Ornamental lighting, an easily variable component of the decor, may help to bridge these contradictory needs, bright and festive or barely aglow, as required.

Here we return to the question raised at the beginning of this essay. The variability of light permits changes in tone, mood, and spirit that can recalibrate an architectural space as well as the stage. At what point do we cease to make any distinction between the audience's space and the actor's? What do we gain and lose from enhancing illusion in both areas?

Lighting, and its control, performs another function: preparing us for the performance. The dimming of the house lights tells us to settle down, end conversations, and direct

our attention toward the performance area. This transition can be simple or complex. The flying chandeliers at the Metropolitan Opera are an unmistakable signal that we are leaving the real, stable, earthbound world behind. At Minnesota Orchestra Hall, the dimmer manufacturer was initially unable to meet our specifications for the house lighting controls. In this project, part of the lighting system illuminates the ceiling, which is a three-dimensional pattern of geometric solid forms. Instead of dimming all the lighting smoothly and in synchronism, the instruction to lower the house lights caused the ceiling lighting to get brighter, briefly, before dimming down. The effect was magical! By behaving perversely, the lighting accentuated the transition between hubbub and hush. When the technical defect was repaired, we programmed the dimmer system to reproduce it.

This was a heightened, theatrical, use of light in a theatrical setting. But light is now used in this way everywhere. Even our homes are fitted with dimmers and tracks filled with spotlights, derived from the theater. One manufacturer of residential lighting has produced a fixture that changes the color of light in a room, according to the user's mood. Is this simply technological trickle-down, or have our domestic needs grown more theatrical, thus requiring such lighting?

Whatever the reason, it is clear that the images, ideas, and techniques that characterized the lighting of theater buildings, and the activities within them, have pollinated (polluted?) our entire built environment and the virtual environment growing within it. The distinction between "real" and "imaginary" is increasingly clouded. That this is an improvement to our quality of life is questionable. This writer believes a civilized society requires both variety and clarity in our constructed world, and that to provide these values we must invent new ways, integrating light and architecture, to "parse" our designs.

Lobby, Boettcher Concert Hall © Norman McGra

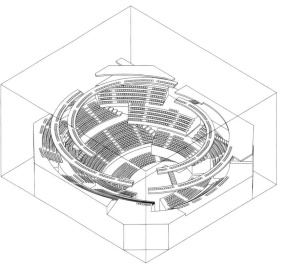

Lobby, Boettcher Concert Hall © Norman McGrath

Auditorium detail, Boettcher Concert Hall © Norman McGrath

Boettcher Concert Hall © Norman McGrath

Previous page: Auditorium, Boettcher Concert Hall © Norman McGrath

Opposite: Seating tiers, Boettcher Concert Hall © Norman McGrath

Madison Civic Center

State Street façade, Madison Civic Center © Norman McGrath

Addition detail, Madison Civic Center © Norman McGrath

Main entry, Madison Civic Center © Norman McGrath

Crossroads, Madison Civic Center © *Norman McGrath*

Crossroads, Madison Civic Center © *Norman McGrath*

Lobby, Madison Civic Center © Norman McGrath

Crossroads, Madison Civic Center © Norman McGrath

View from crossroads to Madison Art Center, Madison Civic Center
© Norman McGrath

Oscar Meyer Theatre, Madison Civic Center © Norman McGrath

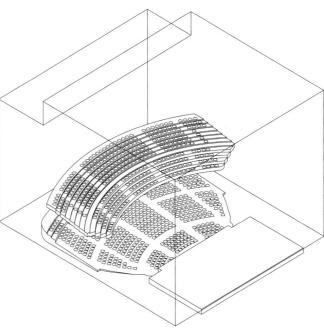

Oscar Meyer Theatre detail, Madison Civic Center © Norman McGrath

Oscar Meyer Theatre auditorium seating, Madison Civic Center © Norman McGrath

Isthmus Playhouse view from balcony, Madison Civic Center © Norman McGrath

Isthmus Playhouse, Madison Civic Center © *Norman McGrath*

Following pages: Isthmus Playhouse view from entry, Madison Civic Center
© *Norman McGrath*

An Actor's Theater

Jane Alexander

A great theater, from an actor's point of view, is one that enhances performance. It is as simple as that. Or as complicated as that. Because the theaters extant today that contribute fully to performance are few and far between. It is a rare architect who consults actors before he designs a theater, and since the actors inhabit the theater space as totally as a family inhabits a home, this is a serious omission.

Each of the performing arts has its own architectural needs. What works for musical theater is not necessarily going to work for spoken drama or comedy. As most of the 100 plays I've been in have been without music, I will attempt to address the needs of actors and the spoken word only.

The creative process for actors, from beginning to end, has never been an easy one; just getting the job is difficult enough. Rehearsal spaces are often woefully inadequate, under- or over-heated, crowded, and badly lit. If necessity is the mother of invention, it is no wonder that an actor's imagination works overtime.

Once the company moves from the rehearsal space to the theater to begin what is known in the trade as "hell week,"—when technical rehearsals begin and the actors meet the sets, costumes, and lighting—the anxiety level increases tenfold. It takes days, sometimes weeks, for an actor to adjust to the full regalia of production, and the architecture of the spaces both onstage and backstage become increasingly important.

I have worked in all kinds of theaters, in many parts of the English-speaking world: the United States, Toronto, London, and Edinburgh. I have performed on thrust-stages, in the round, in black boxes, bowls, pits, and prosceniums large and small. My favorite stages to perform on are the great proscenium theaters built from about 1910 to the early 1920s, which abound on Broadway and in London, and can be found in most older cities of the western world. These theaters often excel acoustically and usually seat fewer than 1,200 people. The sight lines are optimal, allowing a gradual rake in the house and a gentle fan, which always focuses on center stage. These are great conditions for actors, as the audience, seated comfortably and with their attention already concentrated on the stage, can see and hear without strain. The actors' slight elevation above most people seated in the orchestra seats subliminally enhances the importance of the characters, what is said, and the attractiveness of the human figure.

Ideally, every member of the audience should be able to see the actors' eyes. Eyes are "the windows of the soul," and expression and emotion are paramount in an actor's delineation of a role. It's surprising how far emotion can read in a theater when a good lighting designer captures the twinkle or tear in an eye. An actor, of course, conveys character with every sinew of his body, not just the face, which is what makes live theater so much more exciting than film, where the director and the editor select which parts of an actor and his performance to display in each frame.

The proscenium theater heightens focus on the actor in a way that other theaters do not. The problem with a number of the newer proscenium houses, however, is that they are too big for drama or comedy. They are built with too many uses in mind—theater, musicals, and convocations—and end up serving no mistress well.

Acoustically, what works for music can be disastrous for drama, and vice versa. My favorite theaters for acoustics are the Colonial in Boston and the Belasco in New York. In these theaters you can hear a pin drop, quite literally, or a whisper. Although I have come to accept the inevitability of booster microphones on a stage's apron, or hanging above it, I am no fan of body-miking the dramatic actor. The voice registers emotional nuance, and the miked

Spirit Square Arts Center

Existing condition, Spirit Square Arts Center © HHPA

Lobby, Spirit Square Arts Center © Norman McGrath

Addition and renovated façade, Spirit Square Arts Center © Norman McGrath

Glass brick banding, Spirit Square Arts Center © Norman McGrath

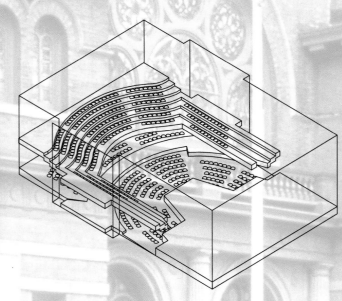

Following page: Auditorium, Spirit Square Arts Center © Norman McGrath

actor on stage is restricted rather than liberated by technical amplification. In musical theater it is more understandable and acceptable, because audiences today are used to controlling amplified music on their home stereos.

The dramatic theater is the domain of the actor and the playwright; the musical theater is the domain of the director and the composer. When pageant becomes important to the writer and director—when the design of the production becomes an equal player with the actors—then theater in the round, or in a large pit or bowl, often serves the vision best. I spent many years performing on the Arena Stage in Washington, DC. Realistic drama such as Chekov, Williams, or Miller was often satisfying there, but epic drama or vaudeville-like pieces worked wonderfully well. O'Neill's The Iceman Cometh, with its many characters' stories taking place in the bar, was compelling in the round, as was Sackler's The Great White Hope, where the metaphor of the arena stage itself resonated in the epic tale of a boxer. Of course, the ancient Greek theaters were all about pageant and event. The audience would spend all day there, soaking up morality as well as drama and spectacle. The large bowl was ideal for this kind of theater, and the acoustics are unparalleled in history. Epidauros, nearly perfect and beautifully preserved, is an acoustical miracle.

My least favorite theaters to play in are those with thrust- or runway-stages. To my mind they are good only for fashion shows, where the audiences' reaction across the way may be as important as the person on display. Black boxes are excellent for small "kitchen dramas," and for trying out experimental works. And small pits are good only if you can't play on any other stage.

An actor spends most of his time in a theater not onstage, but backstage. Too little thought is given to the dressing rooms, the green room, and access to the stage from these venues. It's no mystery that the performers' quarters are traditionally less inviting than the theater owner's office. The money is spent in front of the curtain and not behind it; actors come and go, and there is always someone new waiting in the wings to take over a role. But an actor needs to feel comfortable and adequately prepared for the task at hand.

Dressing rooms need not be immense, but they do need to fulfill basic needs. The first of these is lighting. An actor must have strong incandescent lights surrounding his make-up mirror. Fluorescent lights will not do, and halogen lights are too dangerous; I saw a prop melt away and almost burst into flames when put across the top of a halogen lamp. Second, an actor needs a three-way mirror to check his costume and his look from all sides. An actress I know played a highly emotional scene with a coat hanger hanging from her rear end because she couldn't see the back of her costume beforehand. Funny, to be sure, but not to her!

The green room, as well as the dressing rooms, should have heating and air-conditioning systems that will not damage the vocal cords, and have sufficient soundproofing so warm-ups are possible without bothering others. In addition, some actors absolutely insist on opening windows, so it is important to have a number of rooms on the outside of the building. Sinks must be provided in each dressing room, and toilets and showers nearby. Actors also need to decorate their own spaces with posters, photos, talismans, and the like, so the walls should be malleable in this regard. Access to the stage should be direct and not require a three-minute walk.

An actor's needs are simple: he wishes only to have the audience and himself prepared for the play without distractions. The theater architect is a key player in the event. When he designs a great stage, and the creative talents of playwright, director, designers, and actors connect to the space, there is magic in the theater.

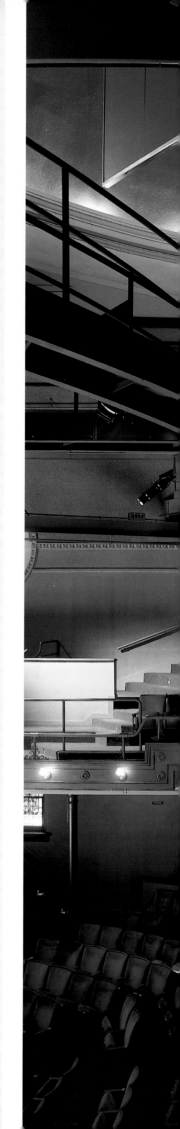

View from balcony, Spirit Square Arts Center © Norman McGrath

View toward stage, Spirit Square Arts Center
© Norman McGrath

Hult Center for the Performing Arts © Timothy Hursley

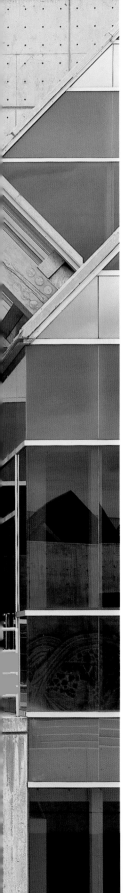

Masks, Hult Center for the Performing Arts
© Timothy Hursley

Multi-level lobby, Hult Center for the
Performing Arts © Norman McGrath

Pedestrian bridge, Hult Center for the
Performing Arts © Timothy Hursley

Lobby roof, Hult Center for the Performing Arts © Norman McGrath

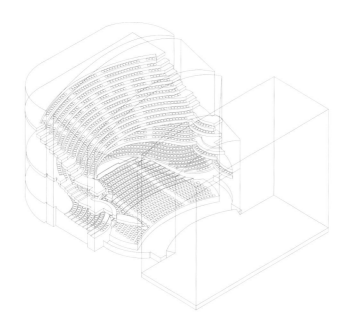

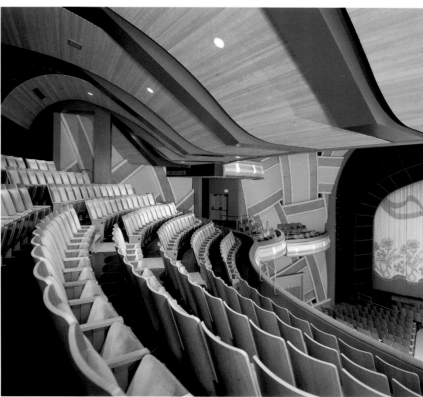

Silva Concert Hall, view from balcony, Hult Center for the Performing Arts © Norman McGrath

63

A View of the Vortex

Eliot Feld

Unencumbered by formal background, education, or credentials and emboldened by a congenital immodesty, I certify that the three principal assets of a proscenium theater, listed in descending order of importance, are GEOMETRY, Geometry, and geometry.

Relative to geometry, all else is essentially frou frou, since the moment we await is the dimming of the house lights to half—the annunciatory pause—and their final dousing to darkness wherein the quotidian is vanquished and the inaugural conceit is revealed as the stage is illuminated. What, then, matters more than the quality of seeing and the quality of hearing, both consequences of angle and distance? Geometry.

And, too, the aperture. The hole in the wall delineated by the proscenium arch; a prefatory halo which celebrates and intensifies our scrutiny of the scene on display. The proscenium opening, a thinking man's rectangle. Geometry.

Your shoulders pinched by Mr. G101 and Mr. G105, Mr. Atlas and Mr. Schwarzenegger, and your knees involuntarily but resolutely wedged by the seat of she who sits directly ahead, a giraffe in aroused bouffant, chapeaued to boot, Ms. F103, who discourteously refuses to remove her head—these, too, are consequences of geometry. Alas, geometry run amok.

In a Euclidean world, one in which geometry prevailed and economics took a back seat, all seats would be created equal, endowed by their creator with certain and inalienable sight lines, and no theater, at least for dance, would exceed 1,200 seats—this to better achieve the unrivaled function of theater architecture, which must be to provide the greatest number, if not all, of the attendees an uninterrupted and felicitous view of the stage, a perch of advantage. To bludgeon the point, you can't see the architecture when the house lights are out. All that remains is the possibility of an ineffable spatial harmony between the viewer and the viewed. And the components of this allusive chord are the confluence of well-tuned geometries.

On the other hand, let me in part rebut the supremacy of geometry by adding that experience need not be pristine to be potent. A mediocre view of an eloquent production beats the hell out of a perfect view of another which is vulgar, driveling, or sentimental.

At age 11, I attended a performance of Petrushka, danced by the Saddler's Wells Ballet at the old Metropolitan Opera House, on 39th Street and Seventh Avenue. From the very last row of the uppermost of several balconies, but fortunately centerish, the ballet below appeared as through a worm hole, made remote by distance, the figures foreshortened by angle. It nonetheless beguiled my child's imagination and remains vivid in memory now, 45 years later.

To coin an aphorism: a theater is become most by most becoming theater. In other words, a good seat ain't a good show.

But back to geometry.

Lighting designers, uniquely beleaguered among theater workers, are mercilessly subject to the opinions, really

Entrance detail, The Joyce Theater
© David Anderson

Entrance from lobby, The Joyce Theater
© Norman McGrath

Previous pages: The Joyce Theater
© Timothy Hursley

The Joyce Theater

Main entrance from street, The Joyce Theater © Christopher Little

Existing Elgin Theater, 1980

Existing Elgin Theater, interior 1980

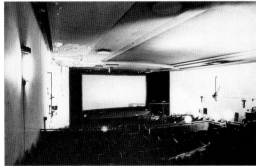

Existing Elgin Theater, interior 1980

improvements, sometimes camouflaged as suggestions, of directors, choreographers, scenic designers, costume designers, divas, and producers as they attempt to do their work in a finite time in a public setting and should not be further aggravated by obtuse geometry. Lighting designers have but three elements with which to work: color, intensity, and angle. Particularly with regard to lighting positions anterior to the proscenium arch (front of house), lighting designers are confounded by irremediable angles too shallow relative to the stage floor. Composition requires control, and angle is a tool of control that services composition by permitting isolation or the desired balance of various things seen simultaneously. Shallow angles are intractably shallow and flummox the gifted most, since artistry is rigorous while ineptness is blithe.

The inutility, nowadays, of an 18th century musical syntax is hardly a denigration of Mozart. So too the macro-geometry of a proscenium theater should reflect the society and technology of its day. Forms are apt when commensurate with their time.

The classical U-shape, with seating boxes hugging supporting outer walls poised commandingly above the hoi polloi below, is, I hypothesize, an expression of the then-present technology used to reinforce a social, political, and economic hegemony. As the aristocracy looked down, conversely, the encompassed rabble looked up at their elevated paternals; a reminder of their dominance. While this design provided some sight-line benefits (though boxes located adjacent to the stage (house right) were deprived of a view stage left and house left deprived of a view stage right), it also provided an excellent vista for the aristocracy to view one another. A panorama of pedigree.

The horseshoe design served a dual purpose. Its geometry provided a view of the stage while reinforcing the social order. Architects knew better than to mess with kings.

An architect today should know better than to mess with the electorate. What was once the power of kings has been minced and divided equally among us. Our societal ideal is now a democratic egalitarianism. As our votes are equal, so too—to the extent that geometry permits—should our seats be equal. As an architectural problem, this is no less nor no more difficult to reconcile than in the world outside the theater. One man, one vote—one man, one seat—each a metaphor for the other. A society without caste requires an egalitarian geometry in which every locus is equal. Though this approach requires some creative geometric hocus pocus, our builders should engage the predicament and assail its impossibility. Whoever said democracy was easy?

Now, for no other purpose than fancy and regalement, imagine an imaginary theater, theoretically, as an aspect of the mind's eye. In designing this space one should consider the inebriating pleasures of "debouchment."

Q: What might bath water feel were it to rise up from the drain, in reverse eddy, into the white enameled expanse of the tub?

A: Delight in unexpected space experienced unexpectedly.

If that seems far-fetched or herniates credulity, try recalling orgasm or birth, whichever you experienced most recently. Exhilaration requires its former confinement.

I posit therefore, that a theater auditorium, our secular temple, be of a scale, volume, and elegance of geometry such that it aggrieves its neighboring spaces. Other public areas are either foyers, coat checks,

or toilets, and functions have inherent hierarchies which should inform the spaces to which they are relegated.

Ideally this theater of the mind would be constructed of nothing. As space alone is immaculate, so the materials that circumscribe and inhabit this volume are necessarily garish by virtue of their materiality.

That which relates to the theater's agenda and serves to remind us of the pre-eminence of performance has a de facto status and its beauty is intrinsic. Bare these trappings, architect: let them hang out and let all else be discrete. Indulge the relevant conceits, beware the irrelevant vanities, address what is needed and delete what is not. Abjure the opulent, riff on the theme if you will, but don't digress. Contrive an intoxicating volume that directs our attention. Remind the congregation whither they came. Construct a modern madrigal. Build a theater that is a paean to its purpose, with the stage as its vortex. Never mind how, just do it!

View from balcony, The Joyce Theater © David Anderson

View from stage, The Joyce Theater © Norman McGrath

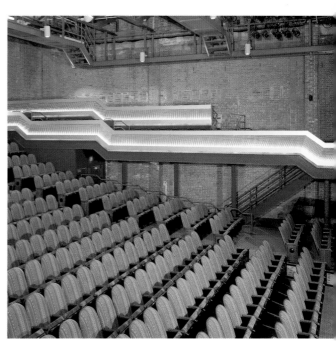

View from balcony, The Joyce Theater © Norman McGrath

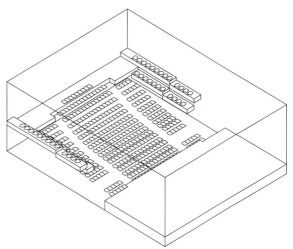

BEING THE BEST OF ALL WORLDS

Douglas Kridler

A theater must be a physically seamless whole; the entire package matters. From its outward appearance to its lobby and auditorium to its technical facilities, a theater defines its community, makes connections to the community's past, and reflects its aspirations. A theater's role as a vessel for congregation and for enabling common experiences is of enormous importance. The sanctity of a theater—the antithesis of the capricious, complicated, and unconsoling experience that the workplace has become—is to be cherished, and is more important now than ever before.

Ah, but can we live up to this beneficent aspiration? Once a theater is designed and built or restored, will its management work to fulfill its potential? Will management have the vision to establish the theater's relevance to the community while using it as a catalyst for urban vitality? Can management realize the theater's spiritual role by welcoming people of all types with varied emotions, stresses, and needs, or will it be the province of a fortunate few? Will the theater's design adequately prepare the audience for the feast that is the performance?

It is true that as we turn to the year 2000 and beyond, theaters are, by and large, the last bastions of a less ubiquitous commercial aesthetic. Corporate logos, while having made it to some marquees, are not yet encroaching on the seating areas of our finest theaters. At least in these we have a safe haven from the relentless pounding of advertising messages.

But managers have an increasingly difficult challenge in front of them. More and more, performing arts venues are finding that they don't have the most comfortable seats, the best sight lines, the most user-friendly policies of all the entertainment facilities available. Theater-goers, with their harried lives, are attracted by movie theaters' stadium seating, state-of-the-art sound systems, cup holders, and customs that allow them to come and go at will to restrooms or refreshment stands, and to clap, laugh, or cry any time they choose. The same goes for sports arenas, with their restaurants, close-in parking, and other amenities. Their luxury suites and personal seat licenses, which replace theater subscriptions, are more likely to attract the corporate entertainment dollar. Social lives are being developed around such places more than ever and, as a result, loyalty to and a sense of ownership in performing arts venues are being eroded.

I believe that theaters' finances will continue to be threatened unless their design is accompanied by inspired, flexible approaches to management. Theaters don't become successful just by opening for business; they do so by earning the respect and enthusiasm of the public. Only then can the goals of architect, planner, and community leader truly be realized.

Night, The Ohio Theatre and Galbreath Pavilion © Cervin Robinson

Façade detail, The Ohio Theatre and Galbreath Pavilion © Cervin Robinson

Entrance, Galbreath Pavilion © Cervin Robinson

Esplanade view to State Capitol, Galbreath Pavilion © Cervin Robinson

Existing auditorium, The Ohio Theatre © Cervin Robinson

Grand stair, view from above, Galbreath Pavilion © Cervin Robinson

Multi-level lobby, Galbreath Pavilion © Cervin Robinson

Handrail detail, Galbreath Pavilion © Cervin Robinson

History, Opera and Theater

Paul Kellogg

Building theaters is not a new art. The basic requirements for the places where mimes, plays, and musical events are performed were already established in the Greco-Roman theaters in Pompeii and Paestum, spaces where we can still walk, haunted by audiences and performers from the second and first centuries B.C. These basic requirements haven't changed: the proscenium—the performance area with flexibility for varying performance and scenic needs; the postscenium—the backstage area for storing scenery, dressing, waiting, and watching in the wings; seating for the audience in raked planes with stepped surrounds; and places where the audience can collect, watch and be watched at intermissions and before and after performances. The Odeon, a 100-seat theater in Pompeii, had a colonnade with a view of Vesuvius for this purpose, and the theater was probably permanently covered so audiences could be protected against external distractions (except Vesuvius itself, sadly) from the necessary suspension of disbelief.

There was sometimes a proscenium arch too, between the audience and the stage—an opening where the everyday world became the imaginative one—because the Greeks and Romans understood that humans need structure to find the way into mystery.

The personnel required to mount an opera performance is daunting: an orchestra, a chorus, principal singers, directors, designers, stage managers, stage hands, and technical and production staff to tend to scenery, costumers, props, lighting equipment, wigs, and make-up. An opera house has to contain all these elements in a fly loft (75 feet high, and potentially overwhelming in a landscape), wings, scene and costume shops, wardrobe rooms, make-up rooms, an orchestra pit, dressing rooms, lighting booths, offices, lighting rails and bridges, and so forth. And that doesn't yet include the audience's needs. A good opera house also has to provide acoustics with balance and presence and warmth, good sight lines, a sense of dramatic intimacy, and reasonable comfort.

Part of the audience experience should include the equivalent of the Pompeian Odeon's colonnade: a promenade area for having a drink and watching our fellows, even without ties and tiaras. The greatest of these I know is in the little opera house in Ghent, with an enfilade of large, beautifully proportioned ornate rooms built for the prosperous burghers of 1830 who could only have looked beautifully proportioned themselves in that space.

There was also, in many of these houses, an order of procession that created (and still creates) excitement, as audiences enter, approaching their seats and the performance, watching the space reveal its surprises.

Glimmerglass Opera already had many of its needs satisfied, if only in the most basic sense, in the high school auditorium where we were performing in 1981, when we first started talking about building a theater for ourselves. But none of what we had was enough.

There weren't enough seats; there wasn't enough backstage space; the stage was too short, too wide, and too low (if the Greeks and Romans built stages for their schools, they probably had the sense not to build them letter-slot shaped); and the atmosphere of ritual inherent in the building, while probably suitable for graduation processions, didn't really fit the

Alice Busch Opera Theater

View toward entry, Alice Busch Opera Theater © Christopher Little

occasion of opera, which includes but is not exclusively the performance.

Especially mindful of the odd appropriateness of our location in deeply rural upstate New York, we wanted to establish a Glimmerglass "experience:" unusual and sophisticated performances in an informal, comfortable, intimate setting. One of our trustees, Eugene Thaw, defined the goal as "a democratic Glyndebourne," which we liked, despite our resistance to comparisons.

We needed 900 seats, which seemed ample, as that would be fifty percent more than we had had in the high school. Our budget required that we keep the number under 1,000 because of the much more expensive code requirements that apply to larger houses. Now, some years later, with most performances selling out, we could wish for a high box-office income potential, but the size we settled on for the Alice Busch Opera Theatre (an average size for European houses for which most opera before 1870 was written) gives us an intimate experience that probably helps attract the full houses we have.

An ornate palace or an egotistical architectural statement would not sit happily on the edge of Lake Otsego, surrounded by working dairy farms and understated upstate Greek Revival and Federal houses.

Upstate prosperity was at its height in the 19th century, and its architecture was the proper starting place for the theater. But the result was much more complex than Greek Revival revival. Nineteenth century dairy barns remain in full use by our roadsides, and abandoned hops barns, with their cupola vents and upright proportions, still rise above century-old lilac stands as reminders of Otsego County's position as the world's leading hops producer of the 1800s. They were the local vernacular inspiration for the exterior, though the influences run

a good deal wider (including Japanese temples), so there are layers of sophistication in the apparently simple facades.

In the same period, opera was at its height as a form of popular entertainment in Europe, with elaborately decorated small opera houses a focus for municipal pride in every city, small and large. This sense of occasion, even in our enthusiasm to break down barriers, was not ignored by Glimmerglass.

Our budget of $6,000,000 wouldn't allow those soaring rooms (even had they been appropriate), but as a summer company we could use the night sky and an open courtyard; if it rains we can have another, more intimate shared experience huddling against nature in the little lobby. (The Greeks would have huddled with nature and worshipped it, but as we aren't Greeks we consider this an "opportunity for growth.")

Because people generally drive to our theater, located eight miles north of a village with no public transportation, the parking lot is the starting place for our procession. A view of the opera house surrounded by meadows across the road, and beyond that a pond which reflects the theater's image with unsettling upside-down accuracy, prepare one for a "through-the-looking-glass" theatrical adventure. A long, curving path (lit later in the evening by lamp poles laden with hops vines) leads around the pond, past an open courtyard with chairs and tables under linden trees, to the outdoor entrance lobby. Inside the house itself, one still doesn't feel enclosed, because the side walls of the auditorium are open to the meadows and courtyard, creating literal and architectural airiness and, as evenings are still bright at eight o'clock, maintaining continuity with the landscape. This is the first surprise: from the front the building seems solid; inside, one senses its lightness.

View toward stage, Alice Busch Opera Theater © Christopher Little

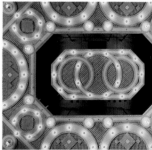

Ceiling, Alice Busch Opera Theater © Christopher Little

View from stage, Alice Busch Opera Theater © Christopher Little

View from balcony, Alice Busch Opera Theater © Elliott Kaufman

But then the next surprise: at curtain time the side walls begin sliding toward the proscenium, enveloping us and bringing attention, briefly, to the room itself, which overhead reveals its 19th century decorative influences (in painted plywood and wooden lattice, not plaster and gilt). But a longer look has to wait for intermission, because the walls have taken all attention irresistibly to the stage. This procession, like a Rossini Act I finale, leaves one full of expectation and delight. It is a great act of architectural manipulation.

We asked for a theater. We got a building that seems alive, a building that is theater in itself—of our time but resonant with the history of its place, of opera, and of 2,200 years of theaters: a building for gathering and celebrating, which takes you into another world.

Renovated street façade, BAM Majestic Theater © Christopher Lovi

Existing conditions, BAM Majestic Theater © David Epstein

Brooklyn Academy of Music, Majestic Theater

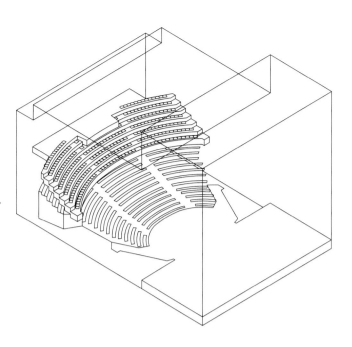

Renovated interior, BAM Majestic Theater © David Epstein

Existing conditions interior, BAM Majestic Theater © David Epstein

85

Doorway, BAM Majestic Theater © Peter Aaron/Esto

View from balcony, BAM Majestic Theater © Durston Saylor

View of orchestra level seating with balcony above, BAM Majestic Theater © Peter Aaron/Esto

AWAKEN THE SPIRIT

Harvey Lichtenstein

I remember how people reacted when they first saw the BAM Majestic Theater. Many were surprised and some even shocked by its unfinished look. Others, used to "new" theaters, were put off by it. A New York Times critic thought it was "precious." Others got it. I remember Teresa Stratas asking me when it was going to be finished, and when I told her that it was finished, she breathed a sigh of relief.

I used to think only of what was on the stage. But it is a two-way street. Coming to the theater is not easy. Everything conspires to make you feel disconnected or distracted; sometimes you are just plain tired. The theater exists to awaken the spirit, and that process should begin as soon as you enter.

What I love about the Majestic Theater is how alive it feels when you walk in; how your interest is awakened as you scan the walls, the pillars, the ceiling, the boxes. There is a palpable energy and vibration. I enjoy looking at the stage and the back wall of the stages but, more importantly, performers tell me how connected they feel to the audience. A theater that facilitates and intensifies that coming together of performer and audience is what you want.

Brooklyn Academy of Music circa 1920s
© Courtesy of the BAM Archives

BAMcafe

Window detail, BAMcafe © Elliott Kaufman

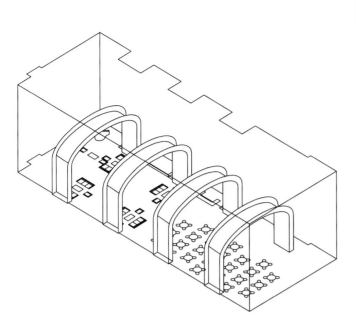

Lounge seating, BAMcafe © Elliott Kaufman

BAM Rose Cinemas

Accessway, BAM Rose Cinemas © Whitney Cox

Accessway, BAM Rose Cinemas © Whitney Cox

Lobby with new escalator, BAM Rose Cinemas © Elliott Kaufman

3, 300 seats, BAM Rose Cinemas © Whitney Cox

#3, View from screen, BAM Rose Cinemas © Whitney Cox

#2, 156 seats, BAM Rose Cinemas © Whitney Cox

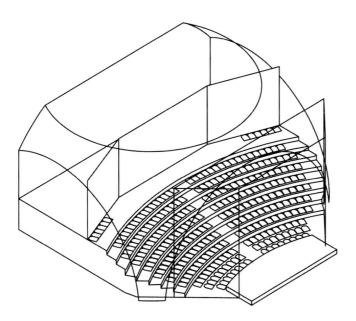

#4, 216 seats, BAM Rose Cinemas © Whitney Cox

South and east façades, Alaska Center for the Performing Arts © Christopher Arend

Opposite: Main entrance, Alaska Center for the Performing Arts © Christopher Little

East façade, Alaska Center for the Performing Arts © Christopher Arend

View of lobby from upper level, Alaska Center
for the Performing Arts © Christopher Little

Colored-glass lobby windows, Alaska Center
for the Performing Arts © Christopher Little

View of lobby from upper level, Alaska Center for the Performing Arts © Christopher Little

Evangeline Atwood Concert Hall, view from balcony, Alaska Center for the Performing Arts © Christopher Little

View of 'Aurora' ceiling from third balcony, Alaska Center for the Performing Arts © Christopher Arend

Proscenium of Evangeline Atwood Concert Hall, Alaska Center for the Performing Arts © Christopher Little

Balcony detail, Evangeline Atwood Concert hall, Alaska Center for the Performing Arts © Christopher Little

Balcony seating, Evangeline Atwood Concert hall, Alaska Center for the Performing Arts © Christopher Little

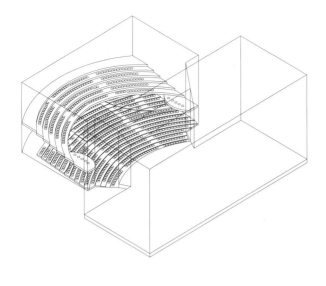

Discovery Theatre ceiling, Alaska Center for the Performing Arts © Christopher Little

Discovery Theatre, Alaska Center for the Performing Arts © Christopher Little

Sydney Lawrence Theatre, Alaska Center for the Performing Arts © Christopher Little

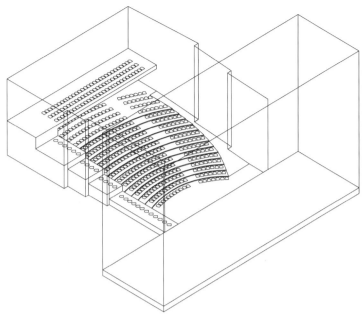

Sydney Lawrence Theatre view towards stage, Alaska Center for the Performing Arts © Christopher Little

LISTENING SPACES
Phyllis Curtin

As a professional singer for 38 years I have performed in opera and recitals, with symphony orchestras and chamber music ensembles, on the stages of theaters, high school auditoriums, art galleries, barns, opera houses, a shed (Tanglewood), concert halls, arenas, and churches. Communication was always the goal and atmosphere an important stimulant (or deterrent) in achieving it.

The best atmosphere for me is a room that seems to be waiting. Standing in a hall before there is an audience, I want to send sound into that expectant space, where music, ideas, emotions, spirit have been at home before me and to which I feel at home adding my music, poetry, characters, devotions. Austere or ornate, the theater is welcoming. Of course acoustics are a major determinant, but the singer on the stage can do nothing at all about that.

I do not know the art of the architect save as it affects me. Teatro Colon in Buenos Aires, Vienna Staatsoper, the Metropolitan Opera House, to give some examples, are warm, friendly rooms in which to work. The Academy of Music in Philadelphia, Symphony Hall in Boston, and, of all things, the Koussevitsky Shed at Tanglewood are thrillingly eager to accept the performer. The Hult Center for the Performing Arts in Eugene, Oregon, smiles encouragingly at the stage, and one is eager to send every best moment of one's work into its embrace. Tsai Performance Space at Boston University accepts cheerfully (an important adverb) a wide variety of activities, including symphony orchestra performance, instrumental and vocal solo recitals, chamber music, and, astonishingly, lectures. The Boettcher Concert Hall in Denver not only expects sound but, for this performer, is entertaining to look into and address.

Style, decor, and shapes can fascinate, please, offend, even distract, but the architectural artist creates a space that brings out the best in the performer while helping the listener concentrate, inside a shell whose design is also determined by style, location, prevailing culture, and a thousand other demands of which I, happily, am unaware.

View towards stage, Boston University, Tsai Performance Space © Steve Rosenthal

Auditorium seating, Boston University, Tsai Performance Space © Steve Rosenthal

Boston University, Tsai Performance Space

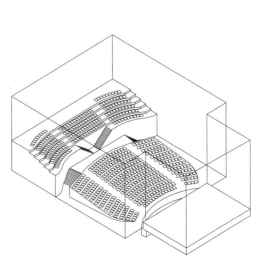

ARCHITECTS AND DESIGNERS: UNIQUE COLLABORATORS

Jennifer Tipton

In these times it is easy to stay at home and still enjoy extraordinary art or entertainment. Our videos and stereos become better and better and the choice is almost limitless. In the immediate future there is promise of bigger screens, greater authenticity of reproduction in both sound and vision, and almost overwhelming variety. Why should we go out to the theater or a concert? The answer is now, as it always has been: that seeing a "live" artist gives an immediacy to the experience of a performance that is like no other thing. An actual performance is different from one viewed on a screen or heard on a cassette player; the performer is on the line. There is no possibility of retaping or cutting and pasting to make a "perfect" performance. The adrenalin that comes from performing live—making mistakes, doing it better than ever before—makes something happen on stage that cannot be recorded.

Any space that houses performance must reflect this experience of the audience in a way that remains true to the performer. A performance is a process of revealing intimate, private accomplishments and feelings in a public forum. The scale of the event will determine the choice of the performance space. The more heightened the production, the grander the venue can be. If the form calls for a full orchestra and chorus as well as principal players, such as a grand opera production, then the stage must be large and, consequently, the audience may be large. If the performers are interested in a style that is more personal, more interior, more "real," then the playing space may be as small and intimate as a living room. In all performance spaces, though, there is an audience "bill of rights" that should be satisfied: every person in the audience should be able to sit comfortably and see and hear clearly.

Since the beginning of theater, people have gone to be seen as well as to see. The building itself can give the audience a sense of excitement. They are in a place where something important is about to happen, and they want it known and remembered that they were there. The setting is as much for the audience as for the stage, and when the architect designs such a building, the auditorium is the background for the audience as foreground. Whatever detail and decoration there is should feature the people within—both the players and the audience.

The building itself will last for many years; the aesthetic of productions presented on the stage may go from one end of the spectrum to the other over the life of that building. The best stage is one that is a "blank slate," whose character is controlled by the creators of the performance and not by the architect. The production on the stage communicates best when it does not fight the building's aesthetic but gains strength from it. If the scenery fights with an ornate proscenium arch, for instance, that battle may become more important than anything that happens in the play, dance, or opera.

The argument between the architect and the creators as to where the line between the audience and the stage is drawn will determine how the audience is affected by the production. The frame of the stage will set up expectations in the viewer or listener. If the frame is designed by the architect, then the creators have another player on the team: one who is not present and is therefore unable to respond to the fluidly changing approach of the director, playwright, composer, or choreographer as they work to find the best way to express their ideas. The best proscenium theaters have a dark area between the house and the stage that makes a clean, non-distracting frame separating the audience from the performers.

North façade, Middlebury College, Center for the Arts © Norman McGrath

Main level lobby, Middlebury College, Center for the Arts © Norman McGrath

View from upper level lobby, Middlebury College, Center for the Arts © Norman McGrath

111

Few of the many large theaters or arts centers in existence today can fill all the seats every night. Should we not consider remaking some of these into several small performance spaces that can provide more kinds of theater to many kinds of audience? It is not just the size of an audience a production attracts that determines the size of the space chosen, but also the way the audience will be involved. Smaller spaces allow a more natural use of the voice and therefore a more natural style of acting or singing. Musical pieces with smaller numbers of instruments and quieter instruments can be heard in smaller spaces without amplification. When the audience is close to the dancer, the physicality of the body becomes as important as the "picture" of the dance. The sense of concentration in the audience members becomes a key element of the production and a major influence on the performers.

There are two types of small space. One, the so-called black box, can be made into anything the designers wish; the other, a living room, library, or private music room, is itself the design for the performance space. In both, the audience is small and is intimately connected to the performance. The audience's presence and participation, even its breathing, become an integral part of what happens on the stage. The performers can be affected by the subtle reactions of the audience members. A performance in such a space can be the seed of a lasting memory, the result of a personal involvement that rarely happens in a larger venue.

Each auditorium has its distinct character, and is an important player in the production. Wherever dreams may take a set or a costume designer, the room where a performance actually takes place will determine, among many things, the scale of the space on stage and the way the audience sees the color of the set and costume. Therefore, the architect becomes a co-designer. The theater house can encourage the lighting designer to imagine extraordinary lightscapes or it can limit the placement of lights, resulting in constant frustration that is stimulating to no one. It is an architect's responsibility to accept the role of partner in hundreds of collaborations, and it is a responsibility that can have a profound effect on the performing arts of the time.

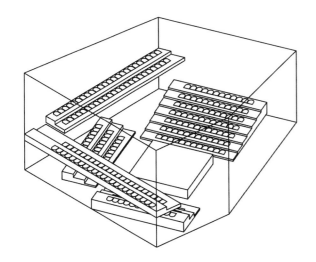

Studio theatre, Middlebury College, Center for the Arts © Norman McGrath

Concert hall view towards stage, Middlebury College, Center for the Arts © Norman McGrath

Concert hall view from side stage, Middlebury College, Center for the Arts © Norman McGrath

Concert hall, Middlebury College, Center for the Arts © Norman McGrath

Dance rehearsal room, Middlebury College, Center for the Arts © Norman McGrath

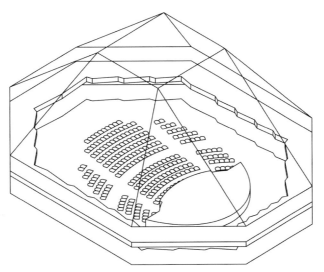

Dance theater, Middlebury College, Center for the Arts © Norman McGrath

University of Nebraska at Omaha, Del and Lou Ann Weber Fine Arts Building

Aerial, University of Nebraska at Omaha, Del and Lou Ann Weber Fine Arts Building © Tom Kessler

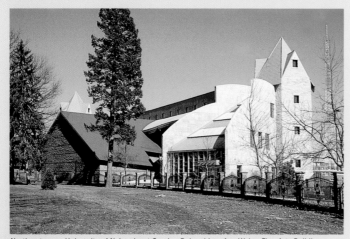

North entrance, University of Nebraska at Omaha, Del and Lou Ann Weber Fine Arts Building © Tom Kessler

East façade, University of Nebraska at Omaha, Del and Lou Ann Weber Fine Arts Building © Tom Kessler

Entrance from main campus walkway, University of Nebraska at Omaha, Del and Lou Ann Weber Fine Arts Building © Tom Kessler

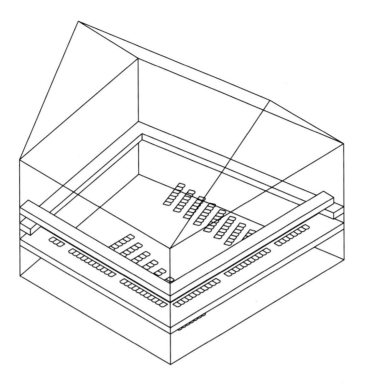

Flexible theater grid level, University of Nebraska at Omaha, Del and Lou Ann Weber Fine Arts Building © Tom Kessler

Costume shop, University of Nebraska at Omaha, Del and Lou Ann Weber Fine Arts Building © Tom Kessler

Dance studio, University of Nebraska at Omaha, Del and Lou Ann Weber Fine Arts Building © Tom Kessler

Doorway detail, University of Nebraska at Omaha, Del and Lou Ann Weber Fine Arts Building © Tom Kessler

Lobby, University of Nebraska at Omaha, Del and Lou Ann Weber Fine Arts Building © Tom Kessler

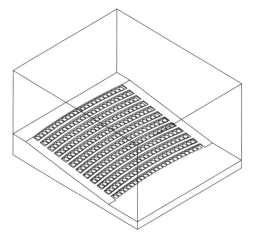

Main entrance at night, Fox Theatres © Christopher Lovi

Concession stand, Fox Theatres © Christopher Lovi

Lobby, Fox Theatres © Christopher Lovi

Cinema, Fox Theatres © Christopher Lovi

THEATER ARCHITECTURE AND SPACE

Robert Whitehead

As a producer and a sometime director, having spent many years struggling with many productions in many theaters, I do not find it easy to discuss my preferences and point of view regarding theater architecture in any specific way. The character of theater production is in constant change and one's thinking, feeling, taste, and imagination are all affected by it. Consequently, the theater one envisions for the needs of a particular production varies as time passes and we seek new forms.

There was a time when I couldn't wait to break out of the proscenium stage and the kind of theater that went with it. At one point I was involved, with Eero Saarinen and Jo Mielziner, in the design of two new Lincoln Center theaters—the Vivian Beaumont and the Mitzi Newhouse—that set out to accomplish this. In the years that followed, I did a number of plays in what is termed a "thrust-stage" theater. I finally came to the conclusion that if such a theater had 1,100 seats or more, it was theatrically effective for many of the classics (particularly the Greeks and the Elizabethans), but had problems relating Moliere, Ibsen, Strindberg, Chekhov, and superior modern (20th century) plays to its height and space. It also seemed this was not the case in the thrust-stage theater of 400 seats or so.

Though I certainly have a personal and subjective reaction to the feeling of warmth, intimacy, and beauty in a theater, I must confess to having no fixed prescription to achieve this perfect form.

I am clear about the needs of a box office and a dressing room, and I certainly appreciate pleasant lobby space. An effective rake in the orchestra-level seats, of course, is conditioned by its relationship to the stage, whether it be a thrust-stage or an ordinary proscenium. In the traditional theater department, for instance, it has always seemed to me that the Ethel Barrymore Theater in New York is about right. Its sight lines are good, the orchestra floor has a pleasant rake, and its relationship to stage level is comfortable. The Lyceum Theater's floor is equally attractive, but in today's economy its seating capacity is too limited. Moreover, the second (upper) balcony changes, not always effectively, the height and sense of space in the theater. Charming as the Music Box Theater is, the stage seems too high, and there is a dip in the first five or six rows of the orchestra floor which never comfortably recovers, as the floor then proceeds to rake its way quietly upward.

The trick in a proscenium house is to solve the problems of sight lines, orchestra width, and relationship to stage level while maintaining an appealing sense of theater and intimacy. This principle applies to houses of 1,400 to 1,500 seats as well as to those with 900 to 1,100 seats. I am absolutely sure that any fully realized, satisfactory theater must have a few rotten seats. None of the theaters in New York has a large enough stage, except possibly the Virginia Theater (originally the Guild), the Lyceum, and the Martin Beck. To a large degree the problem was caused by real estate: the 200-foot New York block.

This restriction does not apply to Lincoln Center. In fact at one point, the board of Lincoln Center nearly turned the stage space of the Vivian Beaumont into a movie house. That space was carefully planned for a large continuing repertory company (London's Royal National Theatre Company), but was never achieved because of lack of funds. Therefore, the stage was never fully utilized for its designed purpose and may as well be a movie theater. As for the Beaumont itself, there are times when I have felt the theater was too large, too spacey, too steeply raked, and too remote from the action. Conversely, I have also felt it had intimacy, warmth, beauty, and a personal connection with the actor and the playwright. I have had the same experience in the Guthrie Theater in Minneapolis, but to a much lesser degree. That theater company has consistently worked toward a certain quality and style, and as a result, the theater itself becomes an important expression of its creative existence. (This theater has about 400 more seats than the Vivian Beaumont.) It is interesting to note that the Beaumont Theater has never, at any time, embraced a program that could make it into a home for an exciting company. Consequently, its architectural success is more open to criticism.

The fact that we are actually discussing the ideals of architectural theater design seems to me, at this moment in history, positive and optimistic. I am so often made to feel that the contemporary theater is almost irrelevant to our present world. The production volume of adventurous playwrighting is forever diminishing, while every city has hundreds of motion picture screens and thousands of TV sets. This situation constantly generates a public and political perception that the living theater is of no importance in our lives.

It is a calamity that our government does not face the responsibility of demonstrating that the theater—as art, education, architecture, tribunal, and, finally, as an expression of what we are as a nation—is of the greatest importance in our lives and in our relationship to the rest of the world.

Punahou School, Dillingham Hall

Restored exterior with new addition, Punahou School, Dillingham Hall © David Franzen

Costume shop, Punahou School, Dillingham Hall © David Franzen

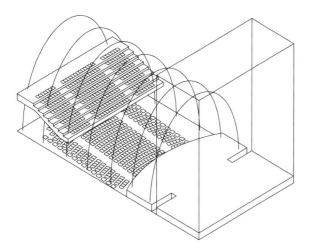

Detail of parabolic arches and catwalk, Punahou School, Dillingham Hall © David Franzen

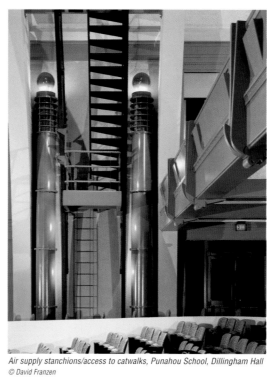

Air supply stanchions/access to catwalks, Punahou School, Dillingham Hall © David Franzen

Orchestra and balcony seating, Punahou School, Dillingham Hall © David Franzen

Existing auditorium, Punahou School, Dillingham Hall
© Hardy Holzman Pfeiffer Associates

LIVING ROOM

Andre Gregory

When we presented Vanya on 42nd Street in the almost bombed-out ruins of the old Victory Theater for a tiny invited audience of friends, Volker Schloendorf, the film director, looked around the dark ruins and said to me, "What a wonderful space—amazing, extraordinary space. I have never seen anything like it. What a wonderful, wonderful space." I told him that I obviously loved the space also but wondered what he found so extraordinary about it. He thought for a moment and replied, "New York is always ahead of its time. New York is always in the avant garde. So while it is true that in Europe the culture is dying, here it is already dead. In this dead culture on this dead street, in this dead theater, what an amazing and peculiar thing, this small group of actors exploring Chekhov—imagine how strange they still care about Chekhov—in front of this peculiar and small audience who also cares—how strange in these times—and behind us in the vast ruins of the auditorium, the ghosts of hundreds of thousands of theater-goers who used to do this every night."

A theme in my work has been the deadening effect of routine and the habitual, and there always seems something musty about the routine of going into the theater, reading our programs, scanning the biographies, waiting for the curtain to go up and the lights to go down. And curtain calls. It all seems terribly predictable. I love to give the audience a sense of the unexpected, the undiscovered, the mysterious, from the first moment they enter a peculiarly appropriate and odd space, especially chosen to suit the nature of the production itself. It's like finding the perfect frame for a painting.

The New Victory Theater

Existing exterior 1992, The New Victory Theater © Addison Thompson

*Opposite: Restored façade along 42nd Street,
The New Victory Theater © Elliott Kaufman*

Restored façade along 42nd Street, The New Victory Theater © Elliott Kaufman

Generally, I develop the work over a rehearsal period of a year or a year and a half, sometimes longer, and then, when the work is finished, find the space—seldom a theater—which seems best suited for the work itself. With Vanya, it was a deserted, abandoned theater. With Alice in Wonderland, it was a mysterious, somewhat nightmarish funhouse—each member of the audience crawled down a large hole to find his or her way into a Fellini-like circus tent. With Endgame, it was an infernal steel machine—the audience and actors both trapped in a cold metallic hexagonal sculpture. When we performed Alice in Iran, we performed in a working class suburb, in an onion and garlic packing factory. The audience sat on fruit crates covered in Persian carpets. A large tree grew through the cement floor that was covered with neighborhood children who'd never been to the theater before.

The audiences for my productions are usually quite small, seldom more than 30. It's not that I am elitist, but I feel that we have been so changed by television and film that we now have a need to see the actor in close-up. I remember going to see The Doll's House on Broadway. I was sitting stage left, in the fourth row in the orchestra. When an actor moved to stage right, I felt as if I were looking down the other end of a football field. It is movies that have done that to us. We want to be up close. At least I do. Even when I go to dance, I like to be in the fourth row—up close. I love to hear the dancers grunting and watch them sweating with the effort of the work. Like at a prize fight. I love the closeness. I love the intimacy.

Grotowski, whose audiences were also very small, once told me that he felt that condemning a production whose audience was small was as condescending as condemning a production whose audience was huge. Of course, interestingly enough,

because of the film version of Vanya, Vanya on 42nd Street, which Louis Malle and I made together, an infinitely larger audience has seen our tiny Vanya than would see a large Broadway musical.

It also seems to me that we are living in times that are no longer communal or familial. We don't have the same sense of social community that we used to. It's easy in an urban environment to feel cut-off and alone. As a result, a space like, say, Carnegie Hall, which used to seem so charming and intimate, now seems to be too large. Just as we can experience or perceive another human being changing at different times of our lives, so too can a fixed space actually change with the times. The actual space of Carnegie Hall is the same, but because of changing conditions it seems much larger.

For the last 30 years, Eugene Lee, one of our greatest scenic designers, has been my collaborator in trying to find the perfect space that seemed appropriate to the work. He is currently working on the environment for Shawn's The Designated Mourner as well as for Shawn's adaptation of The Master Builder. Meanwhile, I am having open rehearsals for The Designated Mourner in my own home, on Perry Street. The performance is in the bedroom and the audience is in the living room.

New lobby stairs, The New Victory Theater © Elliott Kaufman

View from balcony, The New Victory Theater © Elliott Kaufman

View from stage, The New Victory Theater © Elliott Kaufman

Before renovation, The New Victory
Theater © Museum of the City of New York

View of auditorium from upper balcony, The New Victory Theater © Elliott Kaufman

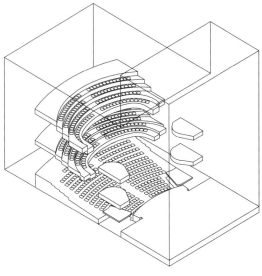

Detail of restored gilded plasterwork, The New Victory Theater
© Elliott Kaufman

Creighton University, Lied Education Center for the Arts

140

Main entrance, Creighton University, Lied Education Center for the Arts © Tom Kessler

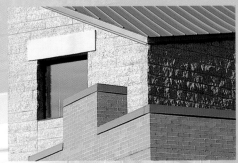

Rooftop detail, Creighton University, Lied Education Center for the Arts © Tom Kessler

Wall details, Creighton University, Lied Education Center for the Arts © Tom Kessler

Piano studio, Creighton University, Lied Education Center for the Arts © Tom Kessler

Stair to balcony, Creighton University, Lied Education Center for the Arts © Tom Kessler

View of auditorium from catwalk, Creighton University, Lied Education Center for the Arts © Tom Kessler

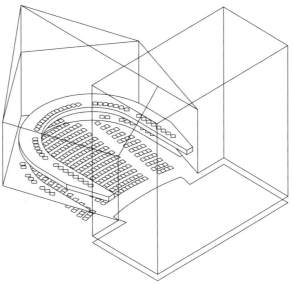

Auditorium, Creighton University, Lied Education Center for the Arts © Tom Kessler

The Hawaii Theatre Center

Two-thirds of 'The Glorification of the Drama' mural, 1990, The Hawaii Theatre Center © David Franzen

Function room, The Hawaii Theatre Center © David Franzen

View of stage from balcony with raised pit lift, The Hawaii Theatre Center
© David Franzen

View looking up at proscenium, The Hawaii Theatre Center © David Franzen

Of Theaters, Players, and Witnesses

Joel Grey

The very first time I went to the theater (I was eight years old), I instantly found it magical, transporting, and utterly transforming. From that day forward, I knew inexorably the following things:

(1) I was to be an actor;

(2) acting would be my life's work;

(3) standing on a stage framed by a reassuring proscenium arch, looking out into the wonderful and mysterious dark, would prove to be the most inevitable, joyous, and natural place to be.

As a result, I was never able to participate in the child–adult charade "And what do you want to be when you grow up?" I was far from grown up, but I never doubted that it was an actor's life for me. Not then, anyway—the doubts came later.

I've always enjoyed being a "witness" as much as a "player." That childhood excitement is with me still. Today the theater's rituals still have the power to draw me into the game. Seeing the marquee and the audience gathering on the street; stepping up to the ticket window; the feel of the tickets, the exchange with the usher who takes them, looks, and sends you to the next usher, who shows you where you'll sit for this "witnessing," then gives you a program (just a quick scan for me, I don't want to know too much); the anticipation of curtain time. I'm already transfixed by the curtain itself. It rustles slightly, piquing my curiosity (what's going on back there?). Then comes the natural quieting of the house, then house lights to half—the resulting anticipation always slightly excruciating— then the nightmare blackout that heralds an experience—surprising, scary, banal,

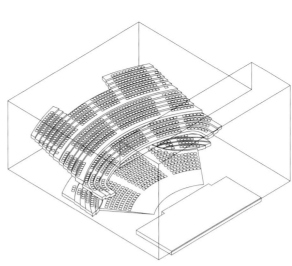

View of box seats from under balcony, The Hawaii Theatre Center © David Franzen

uplifting, or possibly devastating (those times when it's impossible to applaud, impossible to get up from your seat).

For me a curtain's rising is not unlike the onset of a new day—a holy moment that brings two worlds together for the first time: the witnesses and the players, who on this occasion will make of each other what they will, with no guarantees. Everyone steps into the breach—together.

My first awareness of the theater's full power came when, at nine, I was given a leading role in a play at the Cleveland Play House. After a year in the children's theater there (the Curtain Pullers), I landed the juicy role of Pud in On Borrowed Time, by Paul Osborn, on the main stage. It was a heady experience, a fascinating play, and, for my first professional job, I got to work with a superb group of dedicated actors and theater artists. The building itself was beautiful: a dark brick Italianate structure with an entrance of graceful arches, built perhaps in the late 1920s. It housed two architectural gems: the Drury, capacity of 502, and the Brooks, capacity 138. My experience with that company at that impressionable age, I believe, formed my core ideas about the theater and acting and influenced all my future work. At the Cleveland Play House there were rules, ethics, manners, and, above all, respect for the craft. And if you did the work, knew your lines, and had integrity, you were judged favorably and accepted—even if you were only a kid.

I remember that one night each of my parents thought the other was picking me up after a performance. So neither one came. Everyone else left, and I was locked in the theater for a thrilling few hours until I was discovered. I wandered all over the building with nothing more than a romantic

work light, tried on costumes, stood on stage—timidly, then more confidently—spoke Shakespeare's words to an empty house: "I see Queen Mab ..." It was a rare time, and had I not been before, I was then completely hooked.

Today, that experience of standing on a stage, alone, sensing the house, measuring physically and emotionally my place in that particular space, remains an important part of my process. I've always believed that the distance from the stage to the first row has a great deal to do with how easy or difficult a house is to play. And closer is definitely better. When on tour, before going to the hotel from the airport or train station, I would always head straight for the theater—to sense it, size it up, sing or speak a bit of the play to an empty house and align the cells and molecules of me with those of the place.

I've played literally hundreds of theaters, and a few stand out. My favorite musical house is the Broadhurst on West 44th Street in New York. Everything about it is just right: shape, intimacy, color, and, of course, the "rightness" that's not easy to put into words. I adore going to see a play at the Booth on West 45th Street. Most of the big newer houses are problematic. One exception is the performing arts center in Costa Mesa, California. The shape is downright quirky. Upon entering one asks, "Where is the center of the stage? Where is the center of the house?" But by some strange magic, it works beautifully for the players and witnesses alike. Most of the London theaters have the proper atmosphere and spatial rightness.

Great theaters are a gift to actors. I've been a grateful recipient of those gifts for a lot of years, and look forward to all those yet to come.

Box seats, The Hawaii Theatre Center
© David Franzen

View across stage, The Hawaii Theatre Center
© David Franzen

Auditorium wall details, The Hawaii Theatre Center © David Franzen

Proscenium details, The Hawaii Theatre Center
© David Franzen

Restored decorative panels, The Hawaii Theatre Center
© David Franzen

Auditorium dome, The Hawaii Theatre Center
© David Franzen

A House is a Home

Frank Rich

If you hang around a theater long enough, you soon learn to call it "the house." As in:

The house is empty.
The house is open.
The house is full.
The house is closed.
The house is dark.

When I first went to the theater as a child, I didn't know that anyone referred to it as "the house," but I might have guessed as much. It was a house because people lived there. To enter a theater was to be a guest at a surrogate home whose inhabitants included a polite, soft-spoken man who guarded the door, nice ladies in uniforms who took visitors to their seats, and actors who were part of some kind of vicarious family on stage once the curtain went up.

Like any big house, the theater had rooms and whole floors that guests were never invited to see, and whose contents remained mysterious: dressing rooms and wings and cellars entered only through trap doors. Within these hidden chambers moved an extended family of stagehands and dressers and carpenters who kept the house humming and the play moving. The unseen rooms and the invisible magic-makers within them only added to the theater's aura of romance.

As I grew older and learned more about the theater, I discovered that theater buildings come in all shapes and sizes and states of repair. Not all houses are created equal. Not all houses are cared for lovingly by their owners. The best houses are those that fit their occupants. Shakespeare's characters may look adrift in a cavernous hall built for modern musical extravaganzas. The Rockettes would not be at home in the Globe. Plays can be dwarfed by their houses, like a small family rattling around a

Theater seating, The Wilma Theater
© George Golem

Façade along the 'Avenue of the Arts', The Wilma Theater © Matt Warg

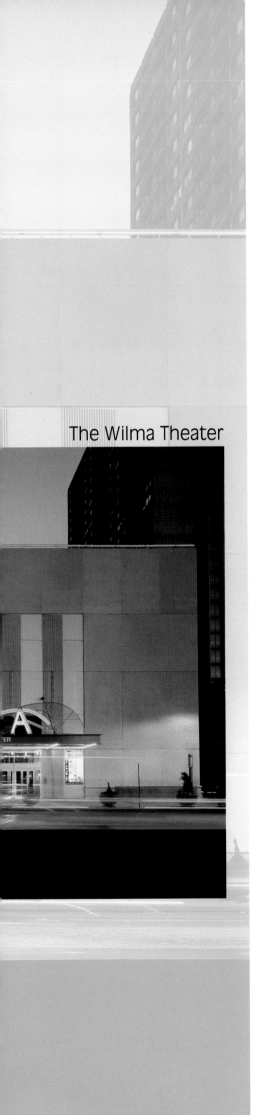

The Wilma Theater

Existing conditions, 1994, New Amsterdam Theatre © Christopher Lovi

New Amsterdam Theatre

Restored marquee on 42nd Street, New Amsterdam Theatre © Disney Enterprises, Inc.

pretentious mansion. Players can combat their houses, if they must struggle to be seen or heard. Though the play's the thing in theater, any drama has an uphill battle if it's performed in a space that doesn't suit it. In contemporary stage design, one of the thorniest challenges is to create a setting that will complement a good house or compensate for the unwanted, distracting theatrics of those houses that loudly assault the eye at the price of being incommodious for their occupants.

No matter how pleasing or wanting their design may be, playhouses, like real houses, are happy places if they're full of happy people, applauding and laughing and cheering. Even the most beautiful house is sad if it's empty. But a tragic house is one that has no show: a dark house. Its marquee will be stripped of names, its front of signs and photos—like a home abandoned by owners who left town in the dead of night, leaving no forwarding address, only a dilapidated "For Sale" sign. If a house remains dark too long, it's a rule of modern commerce that it's likely to be torn down. There are few photographs sadder in the annals of New York City's cultural history than Eliot Elisofon's Life magazine portrait of Gloria Swanson posing as an elegant ghost amidst the ruins of the Roxy Theater, its splintered guts cascading all around her, on the occasion of the movie and vaudeville palace's demolition in 1960.

Great houses have souls. If they can hang on during their dark ages, they can be reborn. Walk into the New Amsterdam Theatre on 42nd Street in New York and you feel the same sense of communal occasion and excitement that greeted audiences who gathered there at the other end of the century. Unlike real houses, the houses where plays once lived are always haunted. When a dark house is reopened, the ghosts of the theater's past raise the voltage on stage just as surely as the theater's marquee lights up the sky.

New Amsterdam Room existing conditions, 1994, New Amsterdam Theatre © Whitney Cox

Opposite: Restored New Amsterdam Room, New Amsterdam Theatre © Disney Enterprises, Inc

Relief of 'Progress' below stained glass skylight, New Amsterdam Theatre © Disney Enterprises, Inc

'Aurora' light fixture, New Amsterdam Theatre © Disney Enterprises, Inc

162

One of four plaster peacocks, New Amsterdam Theatre
© Disney Enterprises, Inc

Reconstructed boxes, New Amsterdam Theatre © Disney Enterprises, Inc

Previous pages: Restored Grand Foyer, New Amsterdam Theatre © Disney Enterprises, Inc

of box seating from balcony © Disney Enterprises, Inc

Refurbished figures atop auditorium dome, New Amsterdam Theatre © Disney Enterprises, Inc

Auditorium existing conditions, 1994, New Amsterdam Theatre
© Whitney Cox

Restored auditorium, New Amsterdam Theatre
© Disney Enterprises, Inc

Detail of wood paneling, New Amsterdam Theatre
© Disney Enterprises, Inc

Detail of elevator door, New Amsterdam Theatre
© Disney Enterprises, Inc

Terra-cotta monkey on banister, New Amsterdam Theatre
© Disney Enterprises, Inc

MUSINGS ON ARCHITECTURE AND THE THEATER: UNLIKELY BEDFELLOWS

Bernard Gersten

Everyone knows theater does not need architecture. Theater needs little more than two planks and a passion. On the other hand, perhaps an architect might be useful: what are the right dimensions for the two planks? What wood might be suitable? And the finish? Paint? Stain? Natural? How best to support them? Sawhorses? Perhaps something in brushed stainless?

Actually, two planks and a passion are just a starting point for a theater. After performing for a while in a two-plank facility, actors yearn for a roof overhead to keep out the rain, the cold, and the sound of airplanes. And if the theater has any success in attracting patronage, in no time at all a convenience or two is called for, and who better than an architect to take the plans to the local building department?

Broadway theater construction, concentrated in the 32 years of the 20th century, with only six new theaters added in the last 70 years, was developer-driven. Architects were provided with painfully inadequate, frequently eccentric footprints, and were cavalierly instructed to shoehorn a theater of maximum capacity into unyielding dimensions. They were routinely forced to sacrifice or compromise foyers, lobbies, box offices, wing space, dressing rooms, and toilets. They couldn't dig deep enough to provide adequate traps and basements; the removal of Manhattan schist was always costly. Theater exit doors and stage loading doors opened directly on to Manhattan's mean streets, and were rarely soundproofed or buffered with interior walls to keep the screaming sirens and grinding garbage trucks (not to mention the historic 44th Street New York Times delivery trucks, especially on Saturday nights) from disrupting any dramatic tension or quiet moment that might have been carefully nurtured on stage.

Architects might have done a great deal for the now historic theaters of New York if it had not been for the restraints imposed by their owners. That so many of the theaters have survived the better part of the century and are still in active use is a tribute to the artisans who designed and built them, to their frequent exterior beauty, even more often to their ornate interiors, and to the superior acoustics with which so many of them were endowed.

In the years following the Second World War, significant numbers of innovative directors became restless with the limitations of proscenium theaters and staging. They began to experiment at not-for-profit, experimental, and Shakespeare theaters across North America. Theater-in-the-Round in Seattle, Circle in the Square, in New York, the Shakespeare festivals in Stratford, Ontario, Connecticut, and New York City, and the Arena Stage, in Wash-ington, all sought to breach the dividing line between stage and audience chamber, to "thrust" the play into the audience's lap, challenging viewers with the immediacy of the plays performed within them, whether by Shakespeare, Osborne, Miller, or Williams.

Perhaps the crest of the revolt against the proscenium occurred in the early 1960s, the precise moment the Vivian Beaumont Theater first appeared on Eero Saarinen's drawing board. The 1,100-seat theater, at Lincoln Center, is in a building that also houses the 300-seat Mitzi Newhouse Theater and the New York Public Library of the Performing Arts. It is arguably the first professional New York City theater to be unencumbered by commercial considerations or limited by Manhattan's

View from stage, Vivian Beaumont Theater, Lincoln Center © Elliott Kaufman

Vivian Beaumont Theater, Lincoln Center

Auditorium, Vivian Beaumont Theater, Lincoln Center © Elliott Kaufman

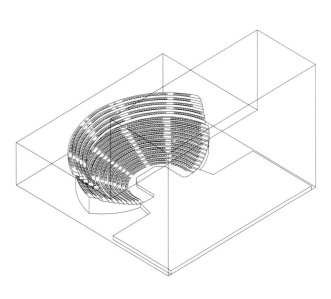

rectilinear street grid. Sited in the northwest quadrant of the 15-acre Lincoln Center campus, a little to the north of the Metropolitan Opera House, the building was allowed to be as long, as wide, as deep, and as high as necessity demanded. No shoehorns were required to squeeze the functions of the two theaters and the unusual demands of a major research library into a masterly Post-Modern structure designed by Saarinen in collaboration with the theater stage designer Jo Mielziner, and built in 1965.

Heralded by an exquisitely proportioned reflecting pool and a stately reclining figure by Henry Moore, the Beaumont building is the most delicate and self-effacing of the Lincoln Center structures. Its glass curtain walls enclose a large and comfortable sub-grade main lobby; patrons entering the south and north doors either disappear from view down the steps as they head for the box office, the rest rooms, or the cafe bar, or are seen climbing the flanking steps to the mezzanine promenade. A cream-white curved wall some 35 feet high conceals the theater within, promising the imminent revelation of its mysteries.

The concept and design of the Beaumont's interior departed from the conventions that inform all Broadway theaters built in the 20th century. They remain traditional proscenium theaters, infinite variations on conventional auditoria, a proscenium stage at one end of the room, and, aligned in slightly curved rows facing the proscenium, as many seats in as many rows in as many sections as footprint and fire laws allow. Boxes and balconies varied by architect and by the shifting fashions that decreed single-balcony theaters to be more economically desirable than two-balcony houses. In the evolving egalitarian United States, there were too few customers who thought their social status earned them only second-balcony seats.

By contrast, Saarinen and Mielziner created a dual-purpose theater that would accommodate the need for a repertory theater at Lincoln Center, rooted in the classics, performing in rotating repertory. The resulting stage was capable of virtually effortless mechanical conversion from proscenium to thrust. But because of sight-line problems with the proscenium configuration, the Beaumont has operated exclusively as a thrust-stage for the past 14 years. Imperfect as they may be, Lincoln Center Theater's two extraordinary theaters and supplemental spaces make it the brightest star in the constellation of New York theaters.

Ideally, theaters representing a wide range of opinions about what a theater ought to be should appear all over the city. This experimenting would contribute to the diversity of the New York theater. But only in the last 25 years or so has the theater begun to take stock of itself and evaluate its relationship to the life of the city, to perceive its singularity, to speculate on its future, to make demands and pursue recognition. Perhaps New York's theaters are its canals, which, despite dire threats and perennial prophecies that the end is nigh, will endure into the 21st century and well beyond. To assure that outcome, the theater will be greatly dependent upon visionary architects who can provide the two planks for the theater's unconquerable passion.

Lobby, Vivian Beaumont and Mitzi Newhouse Theaters at Lincoln Center © Elliott Kaufman

Entrance from parking, Vivian Beaumont and Mitzi Newhouse Theaters at Lincoln Center © Elliott Kaufman

THE AUDIBLE DIFFERENCE

Tony Randall

Theater to me means acting. All the rest is secondary. People try to build theaters for all-purpose use—no good. In my kind of theater, an actor can be heard in the back row (granting a trained voice) without shouting. I hate amplification of the voice. It is unnatural. It puts the actors at one remove and it relieves the audience of the responsibility of listening. This intimacy—people in one room talking and listening—is what a good theater provides. It is not possible in large spaces with the voices coming out of speakers.

I love wood. It feels natural, it's warm, it reflects sound well. The look is inviting and comfortable—a little formal but not too much so. A good theater for post-Ibsen plays (everything written in the last 100 years) should seat fewer than 1,000. The Lyceum and the Music Box are excellent theaters for play acting.

That said, one of the nicest places to see a play in New York City is the Delacorte in Central Park. On a lovely night, with a decent production, you can't ask for a better treat.

The Colburn School of Performing Arts

South façade detail, The Colburn School of Performing Arts © Foaad Farah

Main entrance, The Colburn School of Performing Arts © Foaad Farah

West façade, The Colburn School of Performing Arts © Foaad Farah

Upper level lobby, The Colburn School of Performing Arts © Foaad Farah

Upper level lobby, The Colburn School of Performing Arts © Foaad Farah

Upper level lobby, The Colburn School of Performing Arts © Foaad Farah

Lobby at entry level, The Colburn School of Performing Arts © Foaad Farah

Lobby at entry level, The Colburn School of Performing Arts © Foaad Farah

Auditorium detail, The Colburn School of Performing Arts
© Foaad Farah

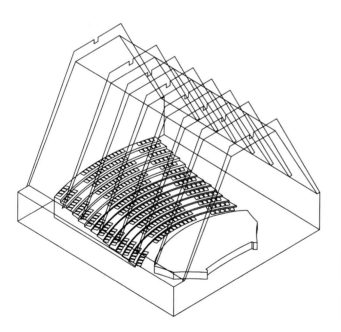

Auditorium balcony, The Colburn School of Performing Arts
© Foaad Farah

Auditorium, The Colburn School of Performing Arts © Foaad Farah

THE ALCHEMY OF ARCHITECT AND ARTIST

Emily Mann

When a theater goes dark for the night, a stagehand leaves a lighted lamp on stage. No one knows why any more, but some old-timers say it is to keep the ghosts away. Others say it lights the stage for the ghosts to play. Whichever theory one adheres to, most theater people agree: a great theater is haunted.

What has this to do with great theater architecture? Everything. Because when one enters a great theater, even if it's new, it must feel seasoned, inhabited by spirits. One senses that electrifying events have happened here and will happen again. When one enters a great theater one feels energy in the air, an extraordinary magical current that only a living space can have. The focus of the auditorium pulls you—eye, heart, mind, imagination—onto the stage.

To prove my point, simply imagine entering your favorite theater—the Moscow Art Theater, the Barrymore, the Joyce—and then think of entering a high school or college auditorium built, say, in the 1960s. None of the excitement I am talking about is there. In the former, your head is light, your heart pounds. In the latter, you have entered what I call a "dead room." Why?

I leave it to the experts to tell you the exact architectural reasons, but as a theater director and writer let me speak simply to a few thoughts. Each theater is unique, and must have a vision behind its form. Key to the vision is the relationship between performer and audience. Some theaters aspire to an intimate connection between audience and actor. Others take a more epic approach. Either can be thrilling when defined carefully, so that every decision bolsters that relationship. Some theaters

Texas Christian University, Mary D. and F. Howard Walsh Center for Performing Arts

Façade detail, Texas Christian University, Mary D. and F. Howard Walsh Center for Performing Arts © David Franzen

Façade facing interior quad, Texas Christian University, Mary D. and F. Howard Walsh Center for Performing Arts © David Franzen

Entry from interior quad, Texas Christian University, Mary D. and F. Howard Walsh Center for Performing Arts © David Franzen

University Avenue entry, Texas Christian University, Mary D. and F. Howard Walsh Center for Performing Arts © David Franzen

Façade facing University Avenue, Texas Christian University, Mary D. and F. Howard Walsh Center for Performing Arts
© David Franzen

View of lobby from upper level, Texas Christian University, Mary D. and F. Howard Walsh Center for Performing Arts © *Craig Blackmon*

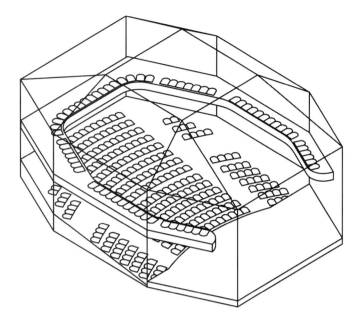

Pepsico Recital Hall, Texas Christian University, Mary D. and F. Howard Walsh Center
for Performing Arts © David Franzen

want the audience to know they are coming to events that will be on-the-edge and dangerous, so that from the moment one enters the lobby or, for that matter, views the outside of the building, one feels that excitement of new, raw work. Other theaters want a feeling of warmth and intimacy, and again, from lobby spaces to auditorium this vision must be carried out. Some want a totally flexible room, where the relationship of actor and audience can change for each event, and others want the perfect proscenium, fixed yet forever changing within that particular form.

Architectural decisions are crucial to realizing these ideas. Each detail must be thought through from the perspective of artist, technician, staff, and audience alike. But at the end of the day, architecture is meaningless—it will not create a real theater—unless a kind of alchemy between architect and artist is present. Finally, what makes a great theater is a mystery. It is not about a beautiful lobby, nor beautifully treated walls, nor even on the shape of the auditorium. It takes wizardry to make a haunted, electric, living theater.

Balcony seating in Pepsico Recital Hall, Texas Christian University, Mary D. and F. Howard Walsh Center for Performing Arts © David Franzen

Pepsico Recital Hall from circulation space, Texas Christian University, Mary D. and F. Howard Walsh Center for Performing Arts © David Franzen

Following pages: Hays Studio Theatre, Texas Christian University, Mary D. and F. Howard Walsh Center for Performing Arts © Craig Blackmon

Vilar Center for the Arts

Skating rink atop Vilar Center for the Arts © Foaad Farah

Auditorium, Vilar Center for the Arts © Foaad Farah

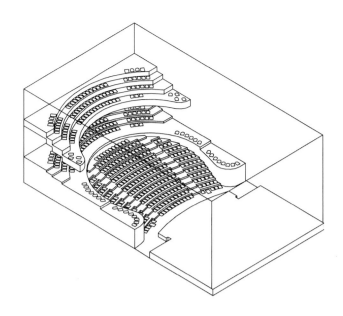

Orchestra and balcony seating, Vilar Center for the Arts © Foaad Farah

Orchestra and balcony seating, Vilar Center for the Arts © Foaad Farah

Orchestra seats, Vilar Center for the Arts © Foaad Farah

Auditorium view from balcony, Vilar Center for the Arts © Foaad Farah

Ramapo College,
Berrie Center for the Performing and Visual Arts

North façade, Ramapo College, Berrie Center for the Performing and Visual Arts © Michael Moran

Façade detail, Ramapo College, Berrie Center for the Performing and Visual Arts © Michael Moran

South façade, Ramapo College, Berrie Center for the Performing and Visual Arts © Michael Moran

AN ARCHITECTURE OF PARTICIPANTS

Robin Wagner

What makes certain theaters so much more desirable than others? What is it about those spaces that capture the imagination of the audience and elicit a near-tangible anticipation? Sometimes you can stand alone, center stage in an empty auditorium, and feel the hush of the house. You might experience a tingling on the back of your neck when the house lights lower and in the moment before the curtain rises. Sometimes it is when the orchestra is tuning their instruments and you sense the conductor's arrival, before he steps up on to the podium, or when the curtain does rise, and you feel a wave of magic spill out into the audience. It is then that you know you are in the house of the muse, when the theater holds you safely in its arms and at the same time fills you with visions of gods and kings, monsters and mayhem; where all the possibilities of the mind can spread out before your incredulous eyes, making you question your very senses. Are you really seeing it? Could it be real? And the answer is "yes, of course it is," and you believe it. It is then that you realize that you are in a sacred space and that anything can happen in this building.

So what makes a space so special? What makes a great cathedral or a great city, for that matter? Is it not a place where the human spirit can be freed? Where the events that happen there are not held captive, but are released into the atmosphere of ideas—where they can reach deeply into the subconscious of humanity, changing us, revealing truths, inspiring us, and, above all, making us feel? Certain forms of these spaces have been with us from the beginning. Anyone visiting the ancient Greek theater at Epidaurus will immediately experience both its vastness and its intimacy,

which includes a phenomenal acoustic clarity. For those of us who speak English, it is perhaps the Elizabethan theater, those oval spaces in which the Shakespearian canon was born, which has left us with a limitless number of conventions that have not only infiltrated our subconscious but have also given birth to practically every artistic device in film, in television, or in the present legitimate theater. The theater of the imagination as described by the chorus of Shakespeare's Henry V allowed the audience to fulfill the vision of the playwright. But the history of spectacle goes back much farther, probably to religious ritual in the dawn of civilization.

Grotowski said, "If you have an actor and an audience of one, you have theater." But what about theater, the place? Is it just wherever the actor performs—space that has evolved because of the nature of the performance? Or can you create a place of anticipation that exists only because of the events that will take place there? It was not until architects brought performance indoors that what we now think of as a theater arrived. Everything that came before had coalesced into a place where life and its events could be redefined, rediscovered, and revealed—a building that could contain all the performing arts.

What is the sense of expectation that is so palpable when you enter a theater? Why is it so much a part of the experience? A simple example is the closed curtain, an ancient device for closing off the playing space; simply raising or removing it can reveal another world, a world of fantasy or perhaps an astonishing vision as suggested by Diagliev in his directive to artists. Or if the curtain is open as the audience arrives, they can adjust to a reality not bound by the artificiality traditionally associated with the stage—a view that implies instead a desire to impart to the viewer a sense of truth, or at least hints that we are not going to try to

Entry level lobby, Ramapo College, Berrie Center for the
Performing and Visual Arts © Michael Moran

Main entrance, Ramapo College, Berrie Center for the Performing and Visual Arts © Michael Moran

fool you into believing you are somewhere other than here. This approach relates to devices used before the invention of the house curtain, in which the arrival of the players began the entertainment.

Across the centuries we have observed many styles of presentation, from the great open-air theaters found in Greece, to the confined courtyard spaces of Spanish classical theater, to those great Elizabethan ovals with platforms open to the sky. The discovery of perspective created a new theater of illusion, in which site-specific places on the stage become more important and the position from which the play was viewed gave new meaning to spectacle. Slowly the fourth wall (the proscenium) began to claim the playwright's vision. We encountered a new stage reality, dependent on the tacit agreement of actor and audience not to acknowledge each other except at certain agreed-upon moments, such as act endings or highly dramatic exits. And so we entered the 20th century with elaborately decorated playhouses that suggested other periods and the majesty of bygone cultures, almost as though what had been on the stage over the centuries was now reflected in concrete and marble. A mirror held up to nature seemed to reflect the great architectural traditions of human history; so much for reality and artifice and the strange juxtaposition of styles that separate the stage from the auditorium.

Now you can choose between one artifice and another. The actor is allowed to create the most thorough illusion of all: what you are seeing is actually happening, the ultimate fusion of writer, performer, and the manipulation of space and vision into what can become theater. Each generation has created its own form of illusion, and as we enter the 21st century we have absorbed a visual sensibility born not only of history but also of film and television—drama of the flat surfaces of observation. We have also made

occasional excursions into the past: arena stages, thrust-stages, removal of prosceniums, and the constant reminders of Brecht that we are in a theater viewing a play. What does it mean? Where are we going? It would seem that the one thing that remains unique in the theater is that it is alive, and therefore the proximity of the audience to the stage is primary. The living theater, where each performance is the only performance, demands a space committed to just that, where the greatest illusions are in the minds of the audience and where, in the 20th century, that wonderful, if antiquated, cube of space known as the stage house continues to offer the most illustrative kind of theater: the theater of spectacle.

Today, however, the theater is less a forum for ideas and more a venue for entertainment. Perhaps it is time to abandon the tall ship-inspired fly chamber and look again into the great sculptural events that we are drawn to and aspire to and are physically able to enter. It may just be that the time has come to re-examine the 18th century baggage we have been dragging along and to reinvent theater for the new millennium, so that it incorporates the intensity and intimacy of drama, the awareness of community, and confrontations that can be found only in the living theatrical experience. Let us make theaters that provoke the imagination, in which anything can happen and does. Let the architect create a place that evokes the vividness of the lives that inhabit it—an architecture of participation, where the slowly evolving events of mankind can define the spaces in which these thrive.

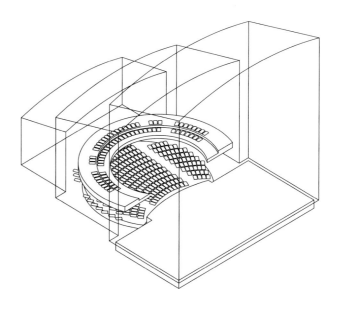

Proscenium theater, Ramapo College, Berrie Center for the Performing and Visual Arts © Michael Moran

Theater lights, Ramapo College, Berrie Center for the Performing and Visual Arts © Michael Moran

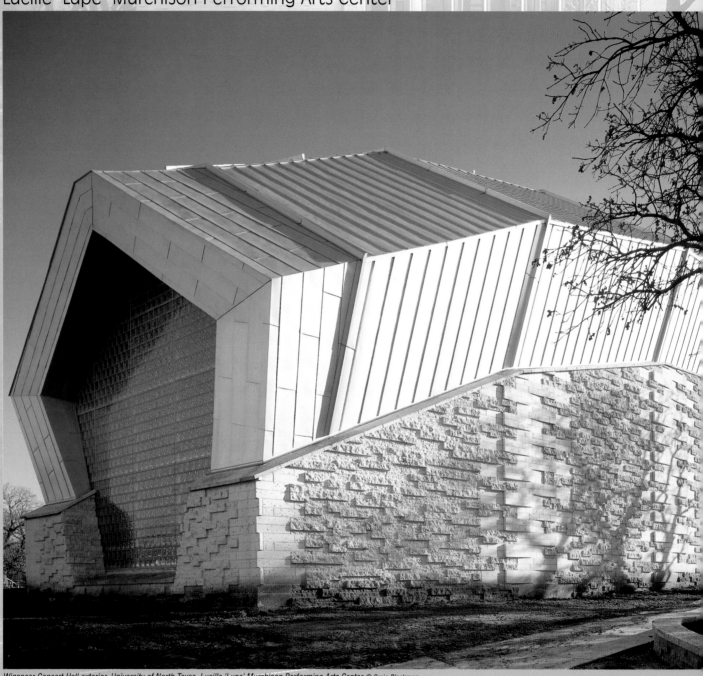

Winspear Concert Hall exterior, University of North Texas, Lucille 'Lupe' Murchison Performing Arts Center © Craig Blackmon

View from Route 95, University of North Texas, Lucille 'Lupe' Murchison Performing Arts Center © Craig Blackmon

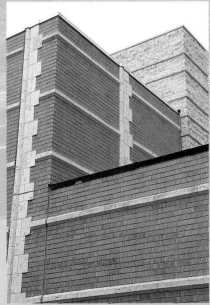

Brick and limestone detail, University of North Texas, Lucille 'Lupe' Murchison Performing Arts Center © Craig Blackmon

ROUSING COLLECTIVE EXPERIENCE

Dave Shrader

There are few "truths" I am comfortable in espousing as an academic administrator, despite more than 25 years of experience. But one must surely be: never, ever suggest a change in a colleague's office space. Never, ever underestimate the emotional connection between personal space and personal identity. Not unless you want a great load of emotion to rain down upon your head.

It seems that every space—every building, every street, every room, every garden—is tied, emotionally and spiritually, to those who contributed to it and those who frequent it, whether they be passers-by, visitors, inhabitants, audience members, or owners. And the greater the personal contact with the space, the greater the emotional connection.

Some of this identification with space carries over to public areas as well. Mass media and the power of American culture seem to be moving us toward a sense of collective self in which every marketplace feels like "home" to us. Sort of. The desperate similarity of such spaces arises, perhaps, from the drive of the marketplace to create universal appetites for ever-new stuff. Whatever the reason, most of our commercial spaces— our shopping malls, factory outlets, dining spaces, product depots—carry with them an unrelenting sameness, more stultifying than comforting.

If such spaces do manage to communicate a sense of self, it is one which is, by design, eternally wanting. Commercial buildings connect people to products. If there were a premise of the marketplace, it would be that happiness is achievable through material acquisition.

Lobby, University of North Texas, Lucille 'Lupe' Murchison Performing Arts Center © Craig Blackmon

West lobby wall, University of North Texas, Lucille 'Lupe' Murchison Performing Arts Center © Craig Blackmon

Public arts spaces tell us who we are and who we might become. But they focus not upon products (although there is certainly growing pressure to do so), but rather upon the processes of human experience. If there were a premise of the arts, it would be that happiness lies in connection with others—past, present, and future.

Our new Winspear Hall, in the University of North Texas's Murchison Performing Arts Center, fosters such connection. The Murchison Center conveys to every person who enters a sense of community that stems neither from the marketplace nor from any narrow personal identity. Instead, it wraps each of us in the warmth of the designer's imagery, which bonds us to each other, to the past, and to the future. It goes far beyond the requirements of technical excellence (which the Murchison Center certainly has in abundance). It is, I think, nothing less than magic.

Lyric Theater. University of North Texas, Lucille 'Lupe' Murchison Performing Arts Center © Craig Blackmon

Winspear Concert Hall detail, University of North Texas, Lucille 'Lupe' Murchison Performing Arts Center © Craig Blackmon

Winspear Concert Hall chandeliers, University of North Texas, Lucille 'Lupe' Murchison Performing Arts Center © Craig Blackmon

Winspear Concert Hall, University of North Texas, Lucille 'Lupe' Murchison Performing Arts Center © Craig Blackmon

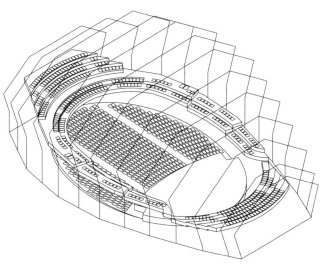

Balcony seating, University of North Texas, Lucille 'Lupe' Murchison Performing Arts Center
© Craig Blackmon

Appendix

Featured Projects

In order of appearance

Simon's Rock College of Bard
Arts Center

Great Barrington, Massachusetts

Simon's Rock College of Bard

Completion 1967

11,000 square feet

140 seats

Playhouse in the Park: Robert
S. Marx Theater

Cincinnati, Ohio

Playhouse in the Park Corporation

Completion 1968

20,000 square feet

629 seats

American Film Institute

Kennedy Center for the Performing

Arts, Washington, DC

American Film Institute

Completion 1973

8,000 square feet

224 seats

American Film Institute

Los Angeles, California

American Film Institute

Completion 1983

8,000 square feet

350 seats (theater); 135 seats
(screening room)

Adelphi University, Robert
G. Olmsted Theater

Garden City, New York

Adelphi University

Completion 1974

19,100 square feet

300 seats

Orchestra Hall

Minneapolis, Minnesota

Minnesota Orchestral Association

Completion 1974 and 1997

90,000 square feet

2,450 seats

Boettcher Concert Hall

Denver, Colorado

The City and County of Denver,

Denver Center for the Performing
Arts,

Denver Symphony Orchestra

Completion 1978

120,000 square feet

2,830 seats

Madison Civic Center

Madison, Wisconsin

The City of Madison

Completion 1980

120,000 square feet

2,200 seats (Oscar Meyer Theatre)

350 seats (Isthmus Playhouse)

Spirit Square Arts Center

Charlotte, North Carolina

Spirit Square Arts Center, Inc.

Completion 1980

100,000 square feet

700 seats

Hult Center for the
Performing Arts

Eugene, Oregon

The City of Eugene

Completion 1982

120,000 square feet

2,487 seats (Silva Concert Hall)

498 seats (Soreng Theater)

The Joyce Theater

New York, New York

Elgin Theater Foundation, Inc.

Completion 1982

17,900 square feet

472 seats

The Ohio Theatre and Galbreath
Pavilion

Columbus, Ohio

Columbus Association for the

Performing Arts

Completion 1984

100,000 square feet

2,779 seats

Alice Busch Opera Theater

Cooperstown, New York

Glimmerglass Opera Company

Completion 1987

12,000 square feet

920 seats

Brooklyn Academy of Music,
Majestic Theater

Brooklyn, New York

The Brooklyn Academy of Music

Completion 1987

35,000 square feet

900 seats

BAMcafe

Brooklyn, New York

The Brooklyn Academy of Music

Completion 1997

20,000 square feet

BAM Rose Cinemas

Brooklyn, New York

The Brooklyn Academy of Music

Completion 1998

14,000 square feet

111, 156, 216 and 300 seats

Alaska Center for the
Performing Arts

Anchorage, Alaska

Municipality of Anchorage

Completion 1988

176,000 square feet

2,078 seats (Evangeline Atwood
Concert Hall)

717 seats (Discovery Theatre)

353 seats (Syndey Lawrence Theatre)

Boston University, Tsai
Performance Space

Boston, Massachusetts

Boston University

Completion 1989

18,000 square feet

576 seats

Middlebury College, Center
for the Arts

Middlebury, Vermont

Middlebury College

Completion 1992

97,000 square feet

370 seats (Recital Hall)

200 seats (Studio Theatre)

145 seats (Dance Theatre)

University of Nebraska at Omaha,
Del and Lou Ann Weber Fine Arts
Building

Omaha, Nebraska

The University of Nebraska at Omaha

Completion 1992

78,500 square feet

250 seats

Fox Theatres

Wyomissing, Pennsylvania

Fox Theatres

Completion 1993

30,000 square feet

125–400 seats (8 theaters)

Punahou School, Dillingham Hall

Honolulu, Hawaii

The Punahou School

Completion 1994

26,000 square feet

653 seats

The New Victory Theater

New York, New York

The New 42nd Street, Inc.

Completion 1995

35,750 square feet

500 seats

Creighton University, Lied
Education Center for the Arts
Omaha, Nebraska

Creighton University

Completion 1996

71,600 square feet

350 seats

The Hawaii Theatre Center
Honolulu, Hawaii

The Hawaii Theatre Center

Completion 1996

37,000 square feet

1,413 seats

The Wilma Theater
Philadelphia, Pennsylvania

The Wilma Theater

Completion 1996

25,000 square feet

296 seats

New Amsterdam Theatre
New York, New York

Disney Development Company

Completion 1997

100,000 square feet

1,814 seats

Vivian Beaumont Theater, Lincoln
Center
New York, New York

Vivian Beaumont Theater, Inc.

Completion 1997

20,500 square feet

1,104 seats

The Colburn School of Performing
Arts
Los Angeles, California

The Colburn School of Performing Arts

Completion 1998

55,000 square feet

420 seats (Concert Hall)

100 seats (Recital Hall)

Texas Christian University, Mary D.
and F. Howard Walsh Center for
Performing Arts
Fort Worth, Texas

Texas Christian University

Completion 1998

56,000 square feet

325 seats (Pepsico Recital Hall)

200 seats (Hays Studio Theatre)

Vilar Center for the Arts
Beaver Creek, Colorado

East/West Partners

Completion 1998

33,000 square feet

530 seats

Ramapo College, Berrie Center for
the Performing and Visual Arts
Mahwah, New Jersey

Ramapo College

Completion 1999

54,000 square feet

350 seats (theater)

100 seats (experimental theater)

University of North Texas, Lucille
'Lupe' Murchison Performing Arts
Center
Denton, Texas

University of North Texas

Completion 1999

72,500 square feet

1,100 seats (Winspear Concert Hall)

400 seats (Lyric Theater)

Chronological List of Theaters

Simon's Rock of Bard College
Arts Center
Great Barrington, Massachusetts
Conversion
1967

New Lafayette Theater II
New York, New York
Renovation
1968

Playhouse in the Park: Robert
S. Marx Theater
Cincinnati, Ohio
New construction
1968

Newark Community Center of
the Arts
Newark, New Jersey
Conversion
1969

Phillips Exeter Academy
Assembly Hall
Exeter, New Hampshire
Conversion
1969

Taylor Theater, Kenan Center
Lockport, New York
Conversion
1969

Dance Theatre of Harlem
School
New York, New York
Conversion
1971

North Carolina School of the
Arts
Winston-Salem, North Carolina
Master plan
1971

Cultural Ethnic Center
Bronx, New York
Conversion
1972

Emelin Theater
Mamaroneck, New York
New construction
1972

Phillips Exeter Academy's
Fisher Theater
Exeter, New Hampshire
New construction
1972

American Film Institute
Kennedy Center for the
Performing Arts
Washington, DC
Conversion
1973

Adelphi University Robert G.
Olmsted Theater
Garden City, New York
New construction
1974

ArtPark
Lewiston, New York
New construction
1974

Orchestra Hall
Minneapolis, Minnesota
New construction
1974

School for the Creative and
Performing Arts
Cincinnati, Ohio
Program and plan to Convert
Cincinnati Union Terminal
1975 (study)

1894 Grand Opera House and
Hotel
Galveston, Texas
Master plan for restoration
1975

North Carolina School of the
Arts
Agnes DeMille Theater
Winston-Salem, North Carolina
Conversion
1975

Feld Ballets/New York
Headquarters and Studios
New York, New York
Conversion
1977

Newark Symphony Hall
Newark, New Jersey
Feasibility study for renovation and
reuse
1977

Annapolis Performing Arts
Center
Annapolis, Maryland
Study for new arts center
1978

Boettcher Concert Hall
Denver, Colorado
New construction
1978

American Center for Students
and Artists
Paris, France
Proposal for restoration and
expansion
1979 (study)

Manhattan Theater Club and
Eastside Playhouse
New York, New York
Plan to link two adjacent theaters
1979 (study)

Strand-Capitol Performing
Arts Center
York, Pennsylvania
Renovation
1979 (study)

Madison Civic Center
Madison, Wisconsin
Renovation, conversion and new
construction
1980

St. Paul's School Music and
Dance Building
Concord, New Hampshire
New construction
1980

Spirit Square Arts Center
Charlotte, North Carolina
Restoration, conversion and new
construction
1980

10 Theaters on 42nd Street
New York, New York
Feasibility of renovating 10 theaters
1980 (study)

American Ballet Theater
Offices and Studios
New York, New York
Renovation
1981

U.S. Army Design Guide for
Music and Drama Centers
Washington, DC
1981

Hult Center for the
Performing Arts
Eugene, Oregon
New construction
1982

The Joyce Theater
New York, New York
Conversion
1982

St. Ann and the Holy Trinity
Brooklyn, New York
Master plan to accommodate
performing arts and religious activities
1982 (study)

Southern Theater
Columbus, Ohio
Plan for restoration and improvement
1982 (study)

Twyla Tharp Dance Company
Studio
Brooklyn, New York
1982 (study)

Will Rogers Memorial Center
Fort Worth, Texas
Master plan
1982

American Film Institute
Los Angeles, California
Campus master plan and renovation
1983

Circle Repertory Theater
New York, New York
Feasibility study for relocation
1983 (study)

National Theater Center
New York, New York
1983 (study)

Spanish Institute
New York, New York
1983 (study)

30 Theaters
New York, New York
1983 (study)

Brooklyn Academy of Music
Brooklyn, New York
Six-phase renovation
1984

Ohio Theatre and Galbreath
Pavilion
Columbus, Ohio
New construction and renovation
1984

University of California at
Davis, Cultural Center
Davis, California
Program and plan
1984 (study)

Warner Performing Arts
Square
Woodland Hills, California
Master site plan and theater
1985 (study)

Yerba Buena Gardens, Center
for Arts and Culture
San Francisco, California
Program for cultural facilities
1985 (study)

Harvard University, Memorial
Hall
Cambridge, Massachusetts
Reuse
1986 (study)

New World Center for the
Performing Arts
Miami, Florida
Plan for new arts center
1986 (study)

Albuquerque Performing Arts
Center
Albuquerque, New Mexico
Program and plan for new arts center
1987 (study)

Alice Busch Opera Theater
Cooperstown, New York
New construction
1987

BAM Majestic Theater
Brooklyn, New York
Reconstruction
1987

The Carolina Theatre
Durham, North Carolina
Renovation and expansion
1987 Design

890 Broadway/Vestron
Pictures
New York, New York
1987 (study)

Middlebury, College Center
for the Arts
Middlebury, Vermont
Master plan
1987

Alaska Center for the
Performing Arts
Anchorage, Alaska
New construction
1988

Liberty and Victory Theaters
New York, New York
Study for non-profit reuse
1988 (study)

Palace West/Orpheum
Theater
Phoenix, Arizona
Plan for restoration
1988 (study)

Paramount Theater at the
Commonwealth Center
Boston, Massachusetts
Reconstruction
1988 (design)

Ahmanson Theater
Los Angeles Music Center
Los Angeles, California
Study for improvements
1989 (competition)

Boston University, Tsai
Performance Space
Boston, Massachusetts
Conversion
1989

Los Angeles County Museum
of Art, Education Center Lecture
Hall
Los Angeles, California
New construction
1989

John Michael Kohler Arts
Center
Sheboygan, Wisconsin
Plan for expansion
1990 (master plan)

Liberty S.P.A.C.E.: Super
Performing Arts Center for
Everyone
New York, New York
Proposal for reuse
1990 (study)

The Broadway Theater
New York, New York
Renovation
1991

Special Attraction Theater
Universal City, California
New construction
1992 (design)

Middlebury College, Center
for the Arts
Middlebury, Vermont
New construction
1992

University of Nebraska, Del
and Lou, Ann Weber Fine Arts
Building
Omaha, Nebraska
New construction
1992

Fox Theatres
Wyomissing, Pennsylvania
New construction
1993

New York Botanical Garden,
Ross Lecture Hall
Bronx, New York
Renovation
1993

Vail Conference Center
Vail, Colorado
Concept development plan for new
construction
1993

Dance Theatre of Harlem
School
New York, New York
Renovation and new construction
1994

Punahou School Dillingham
Hall
Honolulu, Hawaii
Renovation and new construction
1994

University of Southern
California Music School and
Concert Hall
Los Angeles, California
New construction
1994 (design)

Cornell University Bailey Hall
Ithaca, New York
Study for auditorium improvements
1995 (study)

National Actor's Theatre
New York, New York
1995 (study)

The New Victory Theater
New York, New York
Renovation
1995

Union College Yulman
Theater
Schenectady, New York
New construction
1995

University of Minnesota
Northrop Auditorium
Minneapolis, Minnesota
Study for renovation
1995 (study)

Colorado State University/
City of Fort Collins
Performing Arts Center
Fort Collins, Colorado
Study for new arts center
1996 (study)

Creighton University Lied
Education, Center for the Arts
Omaha, Nebraska
New construction
1996

The Hawaii Theatre Center
Honolulu, Hawaii
Master plan and renovation
1996

Palace Theater
New Haven, Connecticut
Study for conversion
1996 (study)

San Diego Civic Theatre
San Diego, California
Study for renovation
1996 (study)

The Wilma Theater
Philadelphia, Pennsylvania
New construction
1996

BAMcafe
Brooklyn, New York
Reuse
1997

Free Theater
New York, New York
1997 (study)

New Amsterdam Theatre
New York, New York
Renovation
1997

New Haven Cultural Arts
District
New Haven, Connecticut
Implementation study
1997 (study)

Orchestra Hall
Minneapolis, Minnesota
Lobby enhancements and theater
upgrades
1997

Vivian Beaumont Theater
New York, New York
Renovation
1997

Brooklyn Academy of Music
BAM Rose Cinemas
Brooklyn, New York
Reuse
1998

California State University,
Fullerton Fine and
Performing Arts Center
Fullerton, California
New construction
1998 (study)

California State University,
Monterey Bay Festival Center
Monterey Bay, California
Master plan for new performing arts
center
1998

Colburn School for
Performing Arts
Los Angeles, California
New construction
1998

Lansing Performing Arts
Center
Lansing, Michigan
New construction
1998 (study)

Omaha Symphony
Omaha, Nebraska
Study for new arts center
1998 (study)

Shubert Organization Theater
at Rock West
New York, New York
Study for new theater
1998 (study)

Tennessee Theatre
Knoxville, Tennessee
Restoration
1998 (study)

Texas Christian University
Walsh Center for Performing
Arts
Fort Worth, Texas
New construction
1998

Vilar Center for the Arts
Beaver Creek, Colorado
New construction
1998

Arena Stage
Washington, DC
Study for renovation and expansion
1999 (study)

Lincoln Center Theaters:
Vivian Beaumont and Mitzi
Newhouse
New York, New York
Lobby enhancements and theater
upgrades
1999

Long Wharf Theatre
New Haven, Connecticut
Programming and master plan for
new theater
1999 (study)

Midland Performing Arts
Center
Midland, Texas
Study for new theater
1999 (study)

Musical Theatre Works
New York, New York
Renovation
1999

Radio City Music Hall
New York, New York
Renovation
1999

Ramapo College Berrie
Center for Performing and
Visual Arts
Mahwah, New Jersey
New construction
1999

Shubert Organization ADA
Study
New York, New York
1999 (study)

Theater for a New Audience
New York, New York
1999 (study)

University of North Texas
Lucille 'Lupe' Murchison
Performing Arts Center
Denton, Texas
New construction
1999

Whitaker Center for Science
and the Arts
Harrisburg, Pennsylvania
New construction
1999

Columbus State University
RiverCenter for the
Performing Arts
Columbus, Georgia
New construction
2000

Hyperion Theater
Anaheim, California
New construction
2000

Lensic Performing Arts
Center
Santa Fe, New Mexico
Renovation
2000

Hippodrome Performing Arts
Center
Baltimore, Maryland
Renovation and new construction
2001

Northwestern University,
Norris University Center Black
Box Theaters
Evanston, Illinois
2001

Princeton University McCarter
Theatre
Princeton, New Jersey
New construction
2001

Shubert Organization Theater
at Theater Row
New York, New York
New construction
2001

University of Notre Dame
Marie P.DeBartolo Performing Arts
Center
South Bend, Indiana
New construction
2002

Project Collaborators

The success of a performance space is dependent upon a collaborative design approach. HHPA has been fortunate to work closely with leading theater technology, acoustic, lighting, and projection consulting firms. Those listed below made significant contributions to the theaters featured in this book, and the buildings' technical sophistication and ease of operation are a direct result of their participation.

Acentech

Acoustic Dimensions, Inc.

Boston Light & Sound, Inc.

Boyce Nemec Designs

Cerami Associates

Cline Bettridge Bernstein Lighting Design, Inc.

The Creative Cinema Company

Fisher Marantz Renfro Stone Inc.

Goodsound Foundation

Paul Gugliotta

Dr. Cyril M. Harris

Horton-Lees Lighting Design, Inc.

Jaffe Holden Scarbrough Acoustics, Inc.

Jerit/Boys, Inc.

Jules Fisher/Joshua Dachs Associates, Inc.

Knudson and Benson

Landry & Bogan

McKay Conant Brook, Inc.

McKinney Technical Services

Norman Russell Design

Chloe Obolensky

Peter George Associates, Inc.

Quentin Thomas Associates

R. Lawrence Kirkegaard & Associates

Robert A. Hansen Associates

Robert Davis, Inc.

Systems Design Associates

Theatre Projects Consultants

Theater Techniques, Inc.

In each theater's region, HHPA has also had the benefit of working with architectural firms who have provided complementary services. Their knowledge of the local context, building methods, urban design criteria, and zoning requirements helped ensure each project's fulfillment, as a positive addition to its community.

The CJS Group Architect Ltd.

Daniel, Mann, Johnson & Mendenhall

Hammel Green & Abrahamson, Inc.

Hecht, Burdeshaw, Johnson, Kidd and Clark, P.C.

KVG Gideon Toal, Inc.

Livingston Slone, Inc.

Lutes/Sanetel Architects

Murphy & Dittenhafer, Inc.

Newman Van Ettan Winfree Associates

Ogburn and Steever

Phillip Markwood Architects, Inc.

Pierce, Segerberg, & Associates

Robert Habel-Hubert M. Garriott & Associates

Rockwell Group

The Schemmer Associates, Inc.

Awards

New Amsterdam Theatre

Award for Preservation Achievement,
Interior Restoration
Victorian Society in America
1998

Award
United States Institute for Theatre
Technology
1998

Award for Interiors
AIA
1998

Interior Architecture Award Citation
AIA, New York Chapter
1998

Lumen Citation
Illuminating Engineering Society,
New York Section
1998

New York Preservation Award
The Municipal Art Society of New York
and Williams Real Estate
1997

New York State Historic Preservation
Award
New York State Office of Parks,
Recreation and Historic Preservation
1997

National Preservation Honor Award
National Trust for Historic Preservation
1997

Excellence in Design Award
New York State Association of
Architects/AIA
1997

The New Victory Theater

Honor Award for Interiors
AIA
1997

Architecture Honor Award
United States Institute for Theatre
Technology
1997

Excellence in Design Award
New York State Association of
Architects/AIA
1996

Brendan Gill Prize
Alliance for the Arts
1995

Punahou School Dillingham Hall

Honor Award for Interiors
AIA
1997

Architecture Merit Award
United States Institute for Theatre
Technology
1997

The Hawaii Theatre Center

Excellence in Design Award
New York State Association of
Architects/AIA
1996

BAM Majestic Theater

Architecture Honor Award
United States Institute for Theatre
Technology
1995

General Excellence for Interior Design
in New York City Award
Interiors Magazine in association with
the National Institute for Architectural
Education
1991

Citation for Architectural Design
New York State Association of
Architects/AIA
1989

Honor Award for Interior Architecture
AIA, New York Chapter
1988

Bard Award of Merit for Excellence in
Architecture and Urban Design
The City Club of New York
1988

Certificate of Merit
Municipal Art Society of New York
1988

Adaptive Use Award
Preservation League of New York
1988

Dance Theatre of Harlem

Award for Excellence in Design
The Art Commission of New York City
1993

University of Nebraska at Omaha, Del and Lou Ann Weber Fine Arts Building

Distinguished Accomplishment in
Architecture Award
AIA, Nebraska Chapter
1993

Honor Award For Innovative
Excellence in Masonry
Nebraska Masonry Institute
1993

The Ohio Theatre and Galbreath Pavilion

James B. Reccie Design Award
Columbus Landmarks Association
1985

Hult Center for the Performing Arts

Lumen Citation
Illuminating Engineering Society
1984

The Joyce Theater

Certificate of Merit
The Municipal Art Society of New York
1983

Award for Excellence
Building Owners and Managers
Association of Greater New York
1983

Citation for Best Interpretive
Reconstruction

Art Deco Society of New York
1983

Bard Award of Merit for Excellence in
Architecture and Urban Design
The City Club of New York
1982

Madison Civic Center

Honor Award for Extended Use for
Excellence in Architectural Design
AIA
1981

Boettcher Concert Hall

Award of Merit
Colorado Masonry Institute
1980

Lumen Citation
Illuminating Engineering Society
1980

Grand Award, Engineering Excellence
Consulting Engineering Council
1980

ArtPark

Excellence in Design Award
New York State Association of
Architects/AIA
1976

Award for Excellence in Environmental
Design
Design & Environment Magazine
1975

Orchestra Hall

Lumen Citation
Illuminating Engineering Society
1975

Playhouse in the Park: Robert S. Marx Theater

Architectural Award of Excellence
American Institute of Steel
Construction
1969

Acknowledgments

This publication is a tribute to the many rewarding working relationships we have enjoyed and the contributions each theater brings to its community. Great theater design requires collaboration. For more than 32 years we have had the pleasure of working closely with many of the creative constituents who bring theater to life.

Paul Latham and Alessina Brooks of The Images Publishing Group Pty Ltd deserve special thanks for their guidance and support, as does Antony Lord and Rod Gilbert for their zestful layout, which wonderfully reflects the essence of our work. We are also beholden to Paul Goldberger, whose preface captures the spirit of this adventure.

The steadfast commitment of our staff in the realization of this publication is of particular note. We would like to thank Debbi Waters for her astute introduction and catalogue of work, as well as for her leadership in the book's production; Susan Packard for her meticulous editing of each essay; and Jessica McCormack for her effort in assembling the photography. Further appreciation goes to Jyh-Ling Lee and Raja Krishnan for their skillful electronic drawings, and to James Brogan, who oversaw their production.

We take great pride in the body of work featured in this volume and salute all HHPA employees, past and present, for their generous talent and dedication to this wide range of accomplishment.

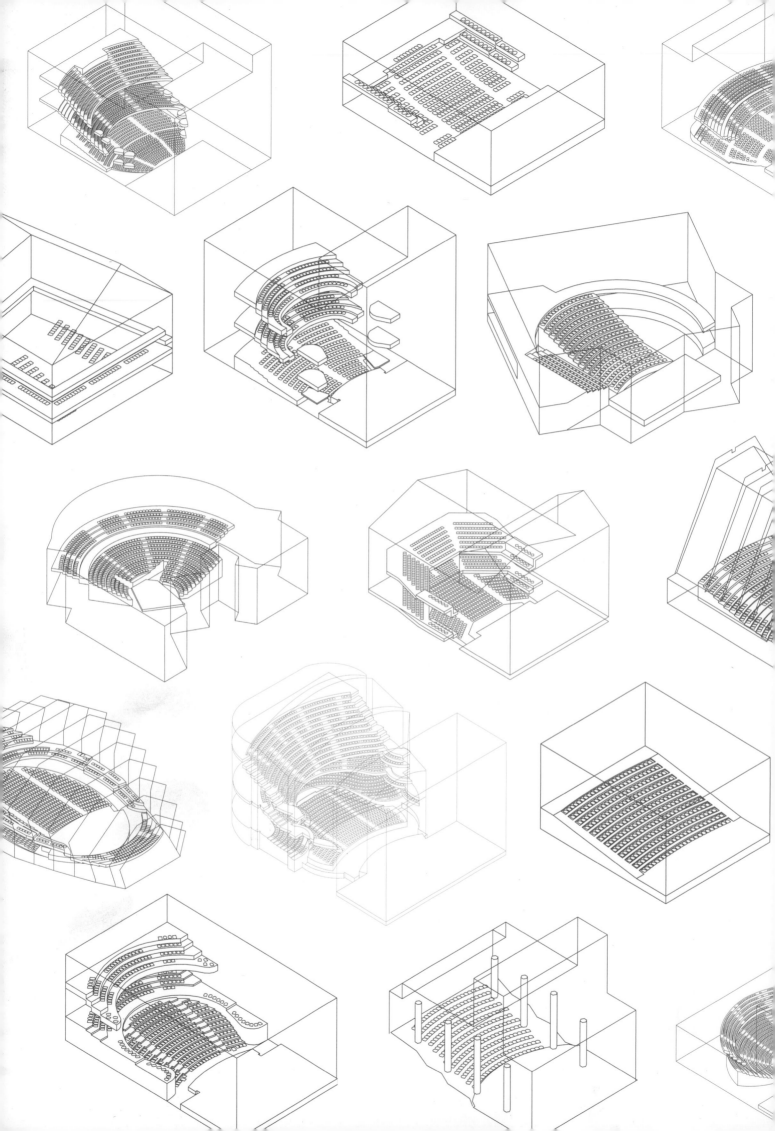